Frequently Asked Questions
in
Islamic Finance

Previously Published Titles by the Author

*Islamic Capital Markets**

*Introduction to Islamic Banking and Finance**

*Islamic Sukuk: a Definitive Guide to Islamic Structured Finance**

Islamic Banking and Finance in the Kingdom of Bahrain,
the Bahrain Monetary Agency

Financial Economics, Financial Times-Prentice Hall.

Economics for Financial Markets, Butterworth-Heinemann

What Drives Financial Markets? Financial Times-Prentice Hall

What Drives the Currency Markets? Financial Times-Prentice Hall

Fed Watching: The Impact of the Fed on the World's Financial Markets,
Financial Times-Prentice Hall

The Valuation of Internet and Technology Stocks, Butterworth-Heinemann

The International Debt Game: a Study in International Bank Lending
(Co-author), Graham and Trotman

A Businessman's Guide to the Foreign Exchange Market,
Graham and Trotman

Monetary Economics, Graham and Trotman

Foreign Exchange Handbook, (Co-author), Graham and Trotman

Gold: An Analysis of its Role in the World Economy, Graham and Trotman

The Finance of International Business, Graham and Trotman

*Available from the author at brian.kettell@islamicbankingcourses.com

Frequently Asked Questions in Islamic Finance

Brian Kettell

A John Wiley and Sons, Ltd., Publication

This edition first published 2010
© 2010 Brian Kettell

Registered office
John Wiley & Sons Ltd, The Atrium, Southern Gate, Chichester, West Sussex, PO19 8SQ, United Kingdom

For details of our global editorial offices, for customer services and for information about how to apply for permission to reuse the copyright material in this book please see our website at www.wiley.com.

A John Wiley & Sons, Ltd. Publication

A catalogue record for this book is available from the British Library.

ISBN 978-0-470-74860-2

Typeset in 9/10.5 Cheltenham-Book by Laserwords Private Limited, Chennai, India.

To my wife Nadia, our son Alexei and daughter Anna. Nadia keeps the whole fleet on an even keel with only the occasional shipwreck.

Contents

Frequently Asked Questions

Preface

*T*he ongoing turbulence in the global financial markets has drawn attention to an alternative system of financial intermediation, Islamic banking and finance. This sector of the financial markets has so far remained on the sidelines of this turbulence. It is a sector which has undergone rapid growth in recent years. Despite this growth the financial community remains largely uninformed as to the key characteristics of the industry. But what exactly is Islamic banking and how does it work? This short text is designed to answer the frequently asked questions almost always raised, by non-specialists, whenever the subject of Islamic banking gets mentioned. It is literally FAQs. Readers seeking more specialised knowledge need to refer to some of my other publications listed earlier.

Even amongst conventional bankers there is much misunderstanding as to what Islamic banking is all about. If you ask a conventional banker what Islamic banking is, he will mumble something about religion. He will then say, 'Well they cannot charge interest but they use something else which is the same thing'. This 'something else', incidentally, is never defined. The banker will then move on to describe Islamic banking as being about smoke and mirrors. To conclude, he will then profoundly announce that, with a few tweaks, it is what he does every day anyway. And that is the end of it.

If pushed to actually describing an Islamic financial instrument or, even worse, to define some Islamic terminology such as Murabaha or Mudaraba, then the banker's eyes will start to gloss over.

Frankly, this stereotyped image is all too prevalent within the banking world. In an endeavour to both enlighten conventional bankers and broaden the understanding of Islamic banking principles these FAQs attempt to answer some of the key issues involved which distinguish Islamic banking from conventional banking.

As the reader will learn, Islamic banking is not about smoke and mirrors. It is in fact about banking based on Islamically ethical principles which are, in many ways, very different indeed from conventional banking principles.

The earliest history of Islamic banking goes back to attempts by Muslim Brotherhood members in the early 1930s to establish Islamic banking in India, an experiment which failed. Egyptian President Gamal Abdel-Nasser shut down the second attempt in 1964, after only one year, later arresting and expelling the Muslim Brothers.

Islamic banking is a banking system that is consistent with the Sharia'a (Islamic law) and, as such, an important part of the system is the prohibition on collecting and paying interest (riba, in Arabic). The Sharia'a also prohibits trading in financial risk because this is seen as a form of gambling, something forbidden in Islam. Another prohibition under the Sharia'a is that Muslims cannot invest in businesses that are considered haram (forbidden or sinful) such as those that sell alcohol and pork, engage in gambling or produce un-Islamic media.

The central religious precept driving the Islamic finance industry is the idea that riba is haram. At first glance, this appears to rule out most aspects of modern finance. But although the Qur'an bans the creation of money, by money, it does allow money to be used for trading tangible assets and businesses - that can then generate a profit.

Consequently, Islamic financial products are designed to create trading or business arrangements that pay profits to investors from business transactions backed by tangible assets, ideally sharing risk and rewards.

The structure of an Islamic bank is radically different from its conventional counterpart. A conventional bank is primarily a borrower of funds on the one hand and a lender on the other. An Islamic bank is rather a partner with its depositors, as well as with entrepreneurs, sharing profit or loss on both sides of the balance sheet.

Another distinction is that a conventional bank would not stop charging interest even if the deployment of its capital fails to bear profit for the entrepreneur, whereas an Islamic bank cannot claim to have a right to profit if the outcome is a genuine loss.

Islamic banks have been operating in places such as Bahrain, Saudi Arabia, Malaysia and Dubai for some time. Conventional bankers have traditionally viewed the sector as a small, exotic niche, focused on household investors. But in the past ten years something extraordinary has occurred behind the scenes.

Several Western investment banks have increasingly started working with Muslim clerics to create a new range of financial products designed for devout Muslims. Somewhat surprisingly, many argue, these have also been welcomed by non-Muslims. The new Islamic banking products range from simple savings schemes or mortgages, to the type of complex capital market products that large corporations and governments use to raise billions of dollars.

Some devout Muslims view this trend with dismay, claiming that it perverts the true spirit of their religion. However, many more welcome it.

Estimates of the size of the Islamic finance industry currently vary wildly from $700 billion to $800 billion. However, whatever the numbers, everyone agrees that the business is expanding rapidly.

The increased demand for Muslim financial institutions in the West has, as mentioned, prompted Western firms to begin providing these services. HSBC, Lloyds Bank, Deutsche Bank, BNP and Citigroup are among the most notable examples of Western firms adapting to tap these new funds.

Introduction

What is Islamic Banking?

What Exactly Is Islamic Banking All About?

Islamic financial institutions are those that are based, in their objectives and operations, on Qur'anic principles. They are thus set apart from 'conventional' institutions, which have no such religious preoccupations. Islamic banks provide commercial services which comply with the religious injunctions of Islam. They provide services to their customers free of interest, (the Arabic term for which is *riba*), and the giving and taking of interest is prohibited in all transactions. This prohibition makes the Islamic banking system differ fundamentally from the conventional banking system.

Technically, *riba* refers to the addition in the amount of the principal of a loan according to the time for which it is loaned and the amount of the loan. In historical times, there was a fierce debate as to whether *riba* relates to interest or usury, although there now appears to be consensus of opinion among Islamic scholars that the term extends to all forms of interest.

The term *riba*, in Islamic law (the *Sharia'a*), means an addition, however slight, over and above the principal. According to the Federal *Sharia'a* Court of Pakistan, this means that the concept covers both usury and interest; that it applies to all forms of interest, whether large or small, simple or compound, doubled or redoubled; and that the Islamic injunction is not only against exorbitant or excessive interest but also against even a minimal rate of interest. Financial systems based on Islamic tenets are therefore dedicated to the elimination of the payment and receipt of interest in all forms. It is this taboo that makes Islamic banks and other financial institutions different, in principle, from their Western conventional counterparts.

There are a range of modern interpretations of why *riba* is considered *haram* (forbidden) but these are strictly secondary to the religious underpinnings.

The fundamental sources of Islam are the Holy Qur'an and the *Sunnah*, a term which in Ancient Arabia meant 'ancestral precedent' or the 'custom of the tribe', but which is now synonymous with the teachings and traditions of the Prophet Mohammed as transmitted by the relaters of authentic tradition (*hadith*). Both of these sources treat interest as an act of exploitation and injustice and, as such, it is inconsistent with Islamic notions of fairness and property rights. While it is often claimed that there is more to Islamic banking than this, such as its contribution towards economic development and a more equitable distribution of income and wealth, its increased equity participation in the economy, and so on, Islamic banking, nevertheless derives its specific *raison d'être* from the fact that there is no place for the institution of interest in the Islamic order.

This rejection of interest poses the central question of what replaces the interest rate mechanism in an Islamic framework. Financial intermediation is at the heart of modern financial systems. If the paying and receiving of interest is prohibited, how do Islamic banks operate? Here, profit and loss sharing (PLS) comes in, substituting for interest as a method of resource allocation and financial intermediation.

The basic idea underlying Islamic banking can be stated simply. The operations of Islamic financial institutions primarily are based on a PLS principle. An Islamic bank does not charge interest but rather participates in the yield resulting from the use of funds. The depositors also share the profits of the bank according to a predetermined ratio. There is thus a partnership between the Islamic bank and its depositors on one side, and the bank and its investment clients on the other side as a manager of depositors' resources in productive uses. This is in contrast with a conventional bank, which mainly borrows funds paying interest on one side of the balance sheet and lends funds, charging interest, on the other. The complexity of Islamic banking comes from the variety (and nomenclature) of the instruments employed, and in understanding the underpinnings of Islamic law.

Six key principles drive the activities of Islamic banks:

1. predetermined loan repayments as interest *(riba)* is prohibited;
2. PLS is at the heart of the Islamic system;
3. making money out of money is unacceptable. All financial transactions must be asset-backed;
4. speculative behaviour is prohibited;
5. only *Sharia'a* approved contracts are acceptable;
6. the sanctity of contracts.

These principles, as applied to Islamic banking and finance, are set out below.

1. Predetermined payments are prohibited

Any predetermined payment over and above the actual amount of principal is prohibited. Islam allows only one kind of loan and that is *qard al hassan* (literally 'good loan') whereby the lender does not charge any interest or additional amount over the money lent. Traditional Muslim jurists have construed this principle so strictly that, according to one Islamic scholar, 'the prohibition applies to any advantage or benefits that the lender might secure out of the *qard* (loan) such as riding the borrower's mule, eating at his table, or even taking advantage of the shade of his wall'. The principle derived from the quotation emphasises that any associated or indirect benefits which could potentially accrue to the lender are also prohibited.

2. Profit and loss sharing

The principle here is that the lender must share the profits or losses arising out of the enterprise for which the money was lent. Islam encourages Muslims to invest their money and to become partners in order to share profits and risks in the business, instead of becoming creditors. Islamic finance is based on the belief that the provider of capital and the user of capital should equally share the risk of business ventures, whether these are manufacturing industries, service companies or simple trade deals. Translated into banking terms, the depositor, the bank and the borrower should all share the risks and the rewards of financing business ventures.

This is unlike the interest-based commercial banking system, where all the pressure is on the borrower: he must pay back his loan, with the agreed interest, regardless of the success or failure of his venture.

The principle, which thereby emerges, is to try and ensure that investments are made into productive enterprises. Islam encourages these types of investments in order that the community may ultimately benefit. However, Islam is not willing to allow a loophole to exist for those who do not wish to invest and take risks but are rather intent on hoarding money or depositing money in a bank in return for receiving interest (*riba*) on these funds for no risk (other than the bank becoming insolvent).

Accordingly, under Islam, either people invest with risk or suffer loss by keeping their money idle. Islam encourages the notion of higher risks and higher returns and promotes it by leaving no other avenue available to investors, the objective here being that high-risk investments provide a stimulus to the economy and encourages entrepreneurs to maximise their efforts to make them succeed, with appropriate benefits to the community.

Risk-sharing

As mentioned above, one of the most important features of Islamic banking is that it promotes risk-sharing between the providers of funds (investors) and the user of funds (entrepreneurs). By contrast, under conventional banking, the investor is assured of a predetermined rate of interest.

In conventional banking, all the risk is borne by the entrepreneur. Whether the project succeeds and produces a profit or fails and produces a loss, the owner of capital is still rewarded with a predetermined return. In Islam, this kind of unjust distribution is not allowed. In pure Islamic banking, both the investor and the entrepreneur share the results of the project in an equitable way. In the case of profit, both share this in pre-agreed proportions. In the case of loss, all financial loss is borne by the capital supplier with the entrepreneur being penalised by receiving no return (wages or salary) for his endeavours.

Emphasis on productivity as compared to credit-worthiness

Under conventional banking, almost all that matters to a bank is that its loan and the interest thereon are paid on time. Therefore, in granting loans, the dominant consideration is the credit-worthiness of the borrower. Under PLS banking, the bank will receive a return only if the project succeeds and produces a profit. Therefore, it is reasoned, an Islamic bank will be more concerned with the soundness of the project and the business acumen and managerial competence of the entrepreneur.

3. Making money out of money is not acceptable

Making money from money is not Islamically acceptable. Money, in Islam, is only a medium of exchange, a way of defining the value of a thing. It has no value in itself, and therefore should not be allowed to generate more money, via fixed interest payments, simply by being put in a bank or lent to someone else.

The human effort, initiative and risk involved in a productive venture are more important than the money used to finance it. Muslim jurists consider money as potential capital rather than capital, meaning that money becomes capital only when it is invested in business. Accordingly, money advanced to a business as a loan is regarded as a debt of the business and not as a capital and, as such, it is not entitled to any return (i.e. interest).

Muslims are encouraged to spend and/or invest in productive investments and are discouraged from keeping money idle. Hoarding money is regarded as being Islamically unacceptable. In Islam, money represents purchasing power, which is considered to be the only proper use of money. This purchasing power (money) cannot be used to make more purchasing power (money) without undergoing the intermediate step of it being used for the purchase of goods and services.

4. Uncertainty is prohibited

Gharar (uncertainty, risk or speculation) is also prohibited.

Under this prohibition, any transaction entered into should be free from uncertainty, risk and speculation. Contracting parties should have perfect knowledge of the counter values (goods received and/or prices paid) intended to be exchanged as a result of their transactions. Also, parties cannot predetermine a guaranteed profit. This is based on the principle of 'uncertain gains' which, on a strict interpretation, does not even allow an undertaking from the customer to repay the borrowed principal plus an amount designed to take into account inflation. The rationale behind the prohibition is the wish to protect the weak from exploitation. Therefore, options and futures are considered as un-Islamic and so are forward foreign exchange transactions, given that forward exchange rates are determined by interest rate differentials.

5. Only Sharia'a approved contracts are acceptable

Conventional banking is secular in its orientation. In contrast, in the Islamic system, all economic agents have to work within the moral value system of Islam. Islamic banks are no exception. As such, they cannot finance any project which conflicts with the moral value system of Islam. For example, Islamic banks are not allowed to finance a distillery, a casino, a night club or any other activity which is prohibited by Islam or is *known* to be harmful to society.

6. Sanctity of contracts

Many verses in the Holy Qur'an encourage trade and commerce, and the attitude of Islam is that there should be no impediment to honest and legitimate trade and business. It is a duty for Muslims to earn a living, support their families and give charity to those less fortunate.

Just as Islam regulates and influences all other spheres of life, so it governs the conduct of business and commerce. Muslims have a moral obligation to conduct their business activities in accordance with the requirements of their religion. They should be fair, honest and just towards others. A special obligation exists upon vendors as there is no doctrine of *caveat emptor* in Islam. Monopolies and price-fixing are prohibited.

The basic principles of commercial *Sharia'a* law are laid down in the four root transactions of:

1. sales (*bay*), transfer of the ownership or corpus of property for a consideration;
2. hire (*Ijara*), transfer of the usufruct (right to use) of property for a consideration;
3. gift (*hiba*), gratuitous transfer of the corpus of property; and
4. loan (*ariyah*), gratuitous transfer of the usufruct of property.

These basic principles are then applied to the various specific transactions of, for example, pledge, deposit, guarantee, agency, assignment, land tenancy, *waqf* foundations (religious or charitable bodies) and partnerships.

Islam upholds contractual obligations and the disclosure of information as a sacred duty. This feature is intended to reduce the risk of asymmetric information and moral hazard. This is potentially a major problem for Islamic banks, and is discussed below.

What Is Asymmetric Information?

This can be defined as information that is known to one party in a transaction but not to the other.

The classical issue here is that some sellers with inside information about the quality of an asset will be unwilling to accept the terms offered by a less informed buyer. This may cause the market to break down, or at least force the sale of an asset at a price lower than it would command if all buyers and sellers had full information. This is known as the 'lemon market' problem in valuation. A lemon, in this context, refers to a poor-quality asset.

This concept has been applied to both equity and debt finance.

For equity finance, shareholders demand a premium to purchase shares of relatively good firms to offset the losses arising from funding lemons. This premium raises the cost of new equity finance faced by managers of relatively high-quality firms above the opportunity cost of internal finance faced by existing shareholders.

In the debt market, a borrower who takes out a loan usually has better information about the potential returns and risk associated with the investment projects for which the funds are earmarked. The lender on the other side does not have as much information concerning the borrowers as he would like.

Lack of enough information creates problems before and after the transaction is entered into. This is potentially a major problem with Islamic profit-sharing financial contracts.The presence of asymmetric information normally leads to adverse selection and moral hazard problems.

Information asymmetry comes in two versions:

1. Adverse selection

This refers to a situation in which sellers have relevant information that buyers lack (or vice versa) about some aspects of product quality. This is the problem created by asymmetric information before the transaction occurs. It occurs when the potential borrowers who are the most likely to produce an undesirable (adverse) outcome. Bad credit risks are those who most actively seek out a loan and are thus most likely to be selected. Again, this is potentially a problem with Islamic profit-sharing financial contracts.

In the simplest case, lenders cannot price discriminate (i.e. vary interest rates) between good and bad borrowers in loan contracts because the riskiness of projects is unobservable. Thus, when interest rates increase, relatively good borrowers drop out of the market, increasing the probability of default and possibly decreasing lenders' expected profits. In equilibrium, lenders may set an interest rate that leaves an excess demand for loans. Some borrowers receive loans, while other, observationally equivalent borrowers, are rationed.

2. Moral hazard

Moral hazard is the consequence of asymmetric information after the transaction occurs. The lender runs the risk that the borrower will engage in activities, described below, that are undesirable from the lender's point of view because they make it less likely that the loan will be paid back.

The conventional debt contract is a contractual agreement by the borrower to pay the lender a fixed amount of money at periodic intervals. When the firm has high profits, the lender receives the contractual payments and the lender does not need to know the exact profits of the borrower. If the managers are pursuing activities that do not increase the profitability of the firm, the lender does not care as long as the activities do not interfere with the ability of the firm to make its debt payments on time. Only when the firm cannot meet its debt payments, thereby being in a state of default, is there a need for the lender to verify the state of the firm's profits.

But if debt interest payments are not being made, as would occur under Islamic financing principles, the moral hazard problem is embedded within the system.

Where Does Asymmetric Risk Come From with Islamic Banking?

The principle of PLS stipulates that the partners are free to determine the extent of their profit-sharing ratio regardless of their capital contributions, with the *Mudaraba* contract (This is described in more detail in Chapter 2). Losses, on the other hand, are to be shared strictly in proportion to their capital contributions. Collateral cannot be provided with PLS activities in the event that the project fails due to business risk. So in the event of the project failing, the Islamic bank is exposed to financial loss. This results in Islamic banks being subject to asymmetric risk.

To ensure timely payment of the loan plus the institution's share of the profits (if any), a fine could be imposed on those borrowers who do not pay on time. To conform with the principles of the *Sharia'a*, these fines must be deposited with a charity, rather than being given to individual financial institutions. So if the borrower defaults, there is no explicit protection for the bank. Again this is asymmetric risk.

Adverse selection refers to the possibility that potential borrowers who are the most likely to produce an undesirable outcome are the ones who more actively seek out a loan, and are thus the most likely to be selected. Moral hazard occurs when the borrower engages in activities undesirable from the lender's perspective, after the loan has been granted.

Since the PLS mechanism emphasises distribution of both risks and profits between the lender and the borrower when a loan is made, the lending institution should, in an ideal world, need only worry about the profitability of the proposed project for which the loan is requested rather than the credit-worthiness of the firm to which they are lending. This should lead to more conservative decisions being made by the lender and to the need for more careful monitoring of the borrower.

In conventional banking, model bank regulation and the availability of deposit insurance have replaced the need for monitoring bank activities by depositors.

Consequently, as far as small depositors are concerned, deposits in one bank are very similar to deposits in another bank, and hence there is less need to monitor bank activities.

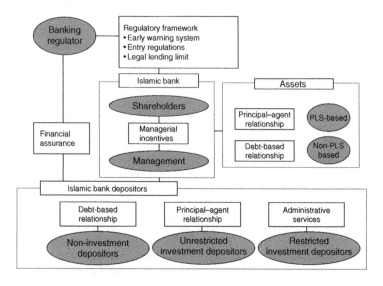

Figure I.1: Relationships within an Islamic banking system. Dar, H.A. and J.R. Presley (1999), Islamic finance: a Western perspective, *International Journal of Financial Services*.

The Islamic, interest-free system, on the other hand, imposes the burden on depositors of gathering information about the safety, soundness, riskiness, and profitability of the bank. Again asymmetric risk is a problem. Figure I.1 illustrates the relationships within an Islamic banking system.

Chapter 1

The Islamic Banking Timeline (1890–2010)

*I*slamic finance has grown to be a US$1 trillion industry, after taking off in the private sector in Gulf States, such as Dubai, in the 1970s.

The *Sharia'a*-law compliant system, which prohibits interest, is the national norm in Sudan and Iran, and in a parallel banking system in Malaysia, Bahrain and a few other Gulf States.

The landmark events in the industry's evolution are summarised here chronologically.

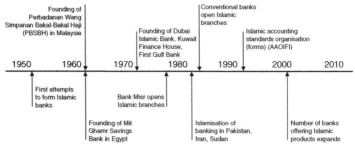

1890s	Barclays Bank opens its Cairo branch to process the financial transactions related to the construction of the Suez Canal. This is understood to be the first commercial bank established in the Muslim world. As soon as the bank's branch was opened, Islamic scholars initiated a critique of bank interest as being the prohibited *riba*.
1900–1930	The critique also spreads to other Arab regions, and to the Indian subcontinent. In this debate, a majority of scholars subscribed to the position that interest in all its forms constitutes the prohibited *riba*.
1930–1950	Islamic economists also initiate the first critique of interest from the Islamic economic perspective and attempt to outline *Sharia'a*-compliant alternatives in the form of partnerships.

1950s	Islamic scholars and economists start to offer theoretical models of banking and finance as a substitute for interest-based banking. By 1953, Islamic economists offered the first description of an interest-free bank based on two-tier *Mudaraba* (both collection of funds and extension of financing on a *Mudaraba* basis). Later they showed that financial intermediation can also be organised on a *Wakala* basis.
1950s–1960s	First experimental Islamic banks develop interest-free savings and loans societies in Pakistan and the Indian subcontinent. Egypt and Malaysia experiment with pioneering ventures in the 1960s. New banks develop during the 1970s as oil money pours into the Gulf states.
1960s	Banking applications and practices in finance based on Islamic principles begin in Egypt and Malaysia. The landmark events include the rise and fall of Mit Ghamr (Egypt) Saving Associations during the period 1961–1964 and the establishment of Malaysia's Tabung Haji in 1962. Tabung Haji has since flourished and has become the oldest Islamic financial institution in modern times.
	Operational mechanisms for institutions offering Islamic financial services (IFS) began to be proposed and a number of books on Islamic banking based on profit and loss sharing/bearing and leasing were published.
1970s	Islamic banks emerge with the establishment, in 1975, of the Dubai Islamic Bank and the Islamic Development Bank (IDB). Also in 1975, *fuqaha* (Muslim jurists) objections to conventional insurance became pronounced, laying the ground for an alternative structure, *takaful*. *Murabaha* was developed as the core mechanism for the investment of Islamic banks' funds.
	Academic activities were launched with the first International Conference on Islamic Economics, held in Mecca in 1976. The first specialised research institution – the Centre for Research in

	Islamic Economics – was established by the King Abdul Aziz University in Jeddah in 1978. The first *takaful* company was established in 1979.
1979	Pakistan becomes the first nation to 'Islamise' banking practices at state level. The process continued until 1985.
1980s	More Islamic banks and academic institutions emerge in several countries. Pakistan, Iran and Sudan announce their intention to transform their overall financial systems so as to be in compliance with *Sharia'a* rules and principles. The governors of central banks and monetary authorities of the Organisation of Islamic Conference (OIC) member countries, in their Fourth Meeting held in Khartoum on the 7th and 8th of March 1981, called jointly, for the first time, for strengthened regulation and supervision of Islamic financial institutions. The Islamic Research and Training Institute (IRTI) was established by the IDB in 1981. In 1980, Pakistan passed legislation to establish *Mudaraba* companies. Other countries such as Malaysia and Bahrain initiated Islamic banking within the framework of the existing system. The International Monetary Fund (IMF) published working papers and articles on Islamic banking, while Ph D research and other publications on Islamic banking were on the increase in the West. The OIC *Fiqh* Academy and other *Fiqh* boards engaged in discussions as to how to apply *Sharia'a* principles to Islamic banks. Islamic mutual funds and other non-banking financial institutions emerged towards the middle of the 1980s.
July 1983	Malaysia opens its first official *Sharia'a*-compliant bank, Bank Islam Malaysia.
September 1983	Sudan reforms its banking system on Islamic principles after President Jaafar al-Numeiri establishes *Sharia'a* law. Dual banking system develops; Islamic in the north and conventional in the south.

March 1984	Iran switches to interest-free banking at the national level after passing a 1983 Islamic Banking law that was promised in the 1979 Islamic revolution.
By 1985	Islamic financial products are offered by more than 50 conventional banks around the globe. Other major banks followed by the 1990s.
February 26, 1990	International Islamic accounting standards organisation, the Accounting and Auditing Organisation for Islamic Financial Institutions (AAOIFI), is established in Bahrain by the IDB.
1990s	Public policy interest in the Islamic financial system grows in several countries.
	The first AAOIFI standards were issued. The development of Islamic banking products intensified. Interest in Islamic finance increased in Western academic circles, and the Harvard Islamic Finance Forum was established. Large international conventional banks started operating Islamic windows. The Dow Jones and Financial Times Islamic indexes were launched. Systemic concerns and regulation, supervision and risk management issues gathered momentum. Several countries introduced legislation to facilitate Islamic banking and its regulation and supervision.
	Commercial event organisers discovered Islamic banking and finance conferences as a source of lucrative business.
1991	Indonesia's first officially sponsored Islamic bank, Bank *Muamalat*, is established.
2000s	Sovereign and corporate *sukuk* as alternatives to conventional bonds emerge and increase rapidly in volume. Bahrain issues Financial Trust Laws.
	International Islamic financial infrastructure institutions such as the Islamic Financial Services Board (IFSB), International Islamic Financial Market (IIFM), General Council for Islamic Banks and Financial Institutions (GCIBFI) and the Arbitration and Reconciliation Centre for Islamic Financial Institutions (ARCIFI), as well as other commercial support institutions such as the International

	Islamic Rating Agency (IIRA) and the Liquidity Management Centre (LMC), were established. The systemic importance of Islamic banks and financial institutions has been recognised in several jurisdictions.
	The governments of United Kingdom and Singapore extended tax neutrality to Islamic financial services.
By 2000	About 200 Islamic financial institutions have over US$8 billion in capital, over US$100 billion in deposits and manage assets worth more than US$160 billion.
	About 40% are in the Middle East, another 40% in South and Southeast Asia and the remaining 20% are split between Africa, and Europe and the Americas.
2001	Malaysia's Financial Sector Master plan sets a target for Islamic finance to make up 20% of the finance sector by 2010. By 2009, its share of financial assets was about 17%.
2002	International standard setting organisation, the Islamic Financial Services Board, is established in Kuala Lumpur, Malaysia.
2004–2008	Investor interest in Islamic finance products grows strongly amid steady rise in oil prices and petrodollars flowing through oil-producing states. World oil prices peaked at over US$147 per barrel in mid-2008 before sliding sharply.
2004	Islamic Bank of Britain, the European Union's first *Sharia'a*-compliant high street bank, opens in the United Kingdom.
2006	Dubai's main stock exchange, the Dubai Financial Market, announces that it is restructuring itself into the world's first Islamic bourse.
2008	Global credit crisis and economic slowdown send conventional financial markets into steep tailspin. New Islamic bond issuance falls two-thirds to a three-year low of US$15.77 billion.

January 2009 Singapore launches the first Islamic bond programme as it vies with Malaysia.

February 2009 Indonesia, the world's most populous Muslim country, sells its first retail *Sharia'a*-compliant bonds, or *sukuk*.

October 2009 The IFC, a member of the World Bank Group, announced it would be the first non-Islamic financial institution to issue *sukuk*.

Late 2009 fears of the first major *sukuk* default emerge but the fears later subside.

Chapter 2

Frequently Asked Questions

What Are the Essential Religious Duties of Muslims?

Answer

The structure of Islam, like any other structure, is founded on pillars. Just as the strength and stability of a structure depends on the strength and stability of its pillars, so does the strength and stability of Islam. Muslims are duty bound to acquaint themselves with the nature of its pillars.

During the 10 years between his arrival in Medina and his death in AD 632, Mohammed laid the foundation for the ideal Islamic state. A core of committed Muslims was established, and a community life was ordered according to the requirements of the new religion. In addition to general moral injunctions, the requirements of the religion came to include a number of institutions that continue to characterise Islamic religious practice today.

Foremost among these were the five pillars of Islam, the essential religious duties required of every adult Muslim who is mentally able. The five pillars are each described in some part of the *Qur'an* and were already practiced during Mohammed's lifetime. They are the profession of faith (*Shahada*), prayer (*Salat*), alms giving (*Zakat*), fasting (*Sawm*) and pilgrimage (*Hajj*).

Although some of these practices had precedents in Jewish, Christian and other Middle Eastern religious traditions, taken together, they distinguish Islamic religious practices from those of other religions. The five pillars are thus the most central rituals of Islam and constitute the core practices of the Islamic faith.

What Is the Shahada?

Answer

The absolute focus of Islamic piety is Allah, the supreme, all knowing, all-powerful, God. The Arabic word *Allah* means 'the God' and this God is understood to be the God who brought the world into being and sustains it to its end. By obeying God's commands, human beings express their recognition of and gratitude for the wisdom of creation, and live in harmony with the universe.

The profession of faith, or witness to faith (*Shahada*), is therefore the prerequisite for membership in the Muslim community. On several occasions during a typical day, and in the saying of daily prayers, a Muslim repeats the profession, 'I bear witness that there is no god but Allah and that Mohammed is his prophet'. There are no formal restrictions on the times and places these words can be repeated.

To become a member of the Muslim community, a person has to profess and act upon this belief in the oneness of God and the prophethood of Mohammed. To be a true profession of faith that represents a relationship between the speaker and God, the verbal utterance must express genuine knowledge of its meaning as well as sincere belief. A person's deeds can be subjected to scrutiny by other Muslims, but a person's utterance of the profession of faith is sufficient evidence of membership of the Muslim community.

What Is Salat?

Answer

The second pillar of Islam is the religious duty to perform five prescribed daily prayers or *Salat*. All adult Muslims are supposed to perform five prayers, preceded by ritual cleansing or purification of the body at different intervals of the day. The Qur'anic references also mention the acts of standing, bowing and prostrating during prayers and facing a set direction, known as *qibla*. The Muslims were first required to face Jerusalem during prayer, but already during Mohammed's lifetime they were commanded to face the *Kaaba*, an ancient shrine in the city of Mecca.

The most detailed descriptions of the rituals for prayer derive from the example set by the Prophet Mohammed and are preserved in later Islamic traditions (*Ahadith*). Some details of these rituals vary. However, all Muslims agree that there are five required daily prayers to be performed at certain times of day: dawn (*fajr* or *subh*), noon (*zuhr*), mid-afternoon (*asr*), sunset (*maghrib*) and evening (*isha*). The dawn, noon and sunset prayers do not start exactly at dawn, noon and sunset; instead, they begin just after, to distinguish the Islamic ritual from earlier pagan practices of worshipping the sun when it rises or sets.

A prayer is made up of a sequence of units called bowings (*rak'as*). During each of these units, the worshipper stands, bows, kneels and prostrates while reciting verses from the *Qur'an*.

Wherever Muslims live in substantial numbers throughout the world, the call to prayer, or *adhan*, is repeated five times a day by a *muezzin* (crier) from a mosque, the Muslim place of worship.

The Friday noon prayer is led by an *imam*, who is a prayer leader. This prayer differs from the usual noon prayers of the other days of the week. As a required part of the ritual at this congregational meeting, two sermons precede the prayer. On other days, Muslims can pray anywhere they wish, either individually or in groups. They must observe the rituals of praying at certain times of day, facing the direction of Mecca, observing the proper order of prayers and preparing through symbolic purification.

What Is Zakat?

Answer

The third pillar of Islam is *Zakat*, or almsgiving. A religious obligation, *Zakat* is considered an expression of devotion to God. It represents the attempt to provide for the poorer sectors of society, and it offers a means for a Muslim to purify his or her wealth and attain salvation. The *Qur'an*, together with other Islamic traditions, strongly encourages charity and constantly reminds Muslims of their moral obligation to the poor, orphans and widows. However, it distinguishes between general, voluntary charity (*sadaqa*) and *Zakat*, the latter being an obligatory charge on the assets or produce of Muslims.

What Is Sawm?

Answer
The fourth pillar of Islam is *sawm*, or fasting. Clear Qur'anic references to fasting account for the early introduction of this ritual practice. The *Qur'an* prescribes fasting during the month of Ramadan, the 9th month of the 12-month Islamic lunar year. The month of Ramadan is sacred because the first revelation of the *Qur'an* is said to have occurred during this month. By tradition the month starts with the sighting of the new moon by at least two Muslims. For the entire month, Muslims must fast from daybreak to sunset by refraining from eating, drinking and sexual intercourse. Menstruating women, travellers and sick people are exempted from fasting, but have to make up the days they miss at a later date.

According to various traditional interpretations, the fast introduces physical and spiritual discipline, serves to remind the rich of the misfortunes of the poor and fosters, through this rigorous act of worship, a sense of solidarity and mutual care among Muslims of all social backgrounds.

What Is the Hajj?

Answer

The fifth pillar requires that Muslims who have the physical and financial ability should perform the pilgrimage, or *Hajj*, to Mecca at least once in a lifetime. The ritual of pilgrimage was practiced by Arabs before the rise of Islam and continues from the early days of Islam.

The *Hajj* is distinct from other pilgrimages. It must take place during the 12th lunar month of the year, known as *Dhu al-Hijja*, and it involves a set and detailed sequence of rituals that are practiced over the span of several days. All of the pilgrimage rituals take place in the city of Mecca and its surroundings, and the primary focus of these rituals is a cubical structure called the *Kaaba*.

According to Islamic tradition, the *Kaaba*, also referred to as the House of God, was built at God's command by the Prophet Ibrahim (Abraham of the Hebrew and Christian Bibles) and his son Ismail (Ishmael).

The *Qur'an* provides detailed descriptions of various parts of the ritual, and it portrays many of these rituals as re-enactments of the activities undertaken by Ibrahim and Ismail in the course of building the *Kaaba*. Set into one corner of the *Kaaba* is the sacred Black Stone, which, according to one Islamic tradition, was given to Ibrahim by the angel Gabriel.

Once pilgrims arrive in Mecca, ritual purification is performed. Many men shave their heads, and men and women put on seamless white sheets. This simple and common dress symbolises the equality of all Muslims before God, a status further reinforced by the prohibition of jewellery, perfumes and sexual intercourse. After this ritual purification, Muslims circle the *Kaaba* seven times, run between al-Safa and al-Marwa, two hills overlooking the *Kaaba*, seven times, and perform several prayers and invocations.

After these opening rituals, the *Hajj* proper commences on the seventh day and continues for the next 3 days. Again, it starts with the performance of ritual purification followed by a prayer at the *Kaaba*. The pilgrims then assemble at Mina, a hill outside Mecca, where they spend the night. The next morning they go to the nearby plain of Arafat, where they stand from noon to sunset and perform a series of prayers and rituals. The pilgrims then head to Muzdalifa, a location halfway between Arafat and Mina, to spend the night. The next morning, the pilgrims head back to Mina, stopping on the way at stone pillars symbolising Satan, at which they throw seven pebbles.

The final ritual is the slaughter of an animal (sheep, goat, cow or camel). This is a symbolic re-enactment of God's command to Ibrahim to sacrifice his son Ismail, which Ibrahim and Ismail duly accepted and were about to execute when God allowed Ibrahim to slaughter a ram in place of his son. (In the Hebrew and Christian Bibles, Abraham is called to sacrifice his son Isaac rather than Ishmael)

Most of the meat of the slaughtered animals is to be distributed to poor Muslims. The ritual sacrifice ends the *Hajj* and starts the festival of the sacrifice, *'id al-adha*. The festivals of breaking fast (*'id al-fitr*) at the end of Ramadan and *'id al-adha* are the two major Islamic festivals celebrated by Muslims all over the world.

During the pilgrimage most Muslims visit Medina, where the tomb of the Prophet is located, before returning to their homes. If the pilgrimage rituals are performed at any time of the year other than the designated time for *Hajj*, the ritual is called *umra*. Although *umra* is considered a virtuous act, it does not absolve the person from the obligation of *Hajj*.

What Is the Sharia'a?

Answer

Sharia'a is an Arabic word meaning the Path to be followed. Literally it means 'the way to a watering place.' It is the path not only leading to Allah, the Arabic word for God, but also believed by all Muslims to be the path shown by Allah, the Creator Himself through His Messenger, the Prophet Mohammed. In Islam, Allah alone is sovereign and it is He who has the right to ordain a path for the guidance of mankind. Thus it is only *Sharia'a* that liberates man from servitude to anyone other than Allah. This is the central reason why Muslims are obliged to strive for the implementation of that path, and no other.

In the *Sharia'a*, therefore, there is an explicit emphasis on the fact that Allah is the Lawgiver and the whole *Ummah*, the nation of Islam, is merely His trustee. It is because of this principle that the *Ummah* enjoys a derivative rule-making power and not an absolute law-creating prerogative. The Islamic State consists of one vast homogeneous commonwealth of people who have a common goal and a common destiny and who are guided by a common ideology in all matters both spiritual and temporal. The entire Muslim *Ummah* lives under the *Sharia'a* to which every member has to submit, with sovereignty belonging to Allah alone.

Every Muslim who is capable and qualified to give a sound opinion on matters of *Sharia'a* is entitled to interpret the law of Allah when such interpretation becomes necessary. In this sense Islamic policy is a democracy. But where an explicit command of Allah or His Prophet already exists, no Muslim leader or legislature, or any religious scholar can form an independent judgement; not even all the Muslims of the world put together have any right to make the least alteration to it.

The executive function, therefore, under the *Sharia'a* vests solely in the just ruler or a group of such people that appoints its delegates and is responsible only to the *Sharia'a* as represented by the Council of Jurists ('*Ulema* and *Fuqaha'*) in whom the legislative function of deriving laws from the Book of Allah and the *Sunnah* is vested. New laws according to the needs of the time and circumstances are only made by these men learned in the guiding principles of law.

But the fundamental principles on which the Islamic legal system rests are that the laws of Islam are not passed in a heated assembly by men who ardently desire the legislation in their own interest against men who ardently oppose it in their own interest. The laws of Islam are firmly based upon the *Sharia'a* and are, therefore deemed to be, in the interest of the people as a whole. They are not the work of warring politicians, but of sober jurists.

The difference between other legal systems and the *Sharia'a* is that under the *Sharia'a* its fountainhead is the *Qur'an* and the *Sunnah*. The *Qur'an* and the *Sunnah* are the gifts given to the entire *Ummah*. Therefore the *Ummah* as a whole is collectively responsible for the administration of Justice.

The other important point in this regard is that under the *Sharia'a*, Justice is administered in the name of Allah.

What Are the Sources of the Sharia'a?

Answer

The ideal code of conduct, or a pure way of life as the *Sharia'a* is thought of by Muslims, has much wider scope and purpose than an ordinary legal system in the western sense of the term. The *Sharia'a* aims at regulating the relationship of man with Allah and man with man. This is the reason why *Sharia'a* law cannot be separated from Islamic ethics. The process of revelation of various injunctions of the *Qur'an* shows that the revelation came down when some social, moral or religious necessity arose, or when some Companions consulted the Prophet concerning some significant problems which had wide repercussions on the lives of Muslims. The *Qur'an* is the main source of the *Sharia'a*.

The scholars of the *Qur'an* have enumerated varying number of verses of legal injunctions, but the number is considered to be approximately 500. They deal with marriage, polygamy, maintenance, rights and obligations of the spouses, divorce and various modes of dissolution of marriage, the period of retreat after divorce, fosterage, contracts, loans, deposits, weights and measures, removal of injury, oaths and vows, punishments for crime, wills, inheritance, equity, fraternity, liberty, justice to all, principles of an ideal, state, fundamental human rights, laws of war and peace, judicial administration and so on.

The Qur'anic injunctions, from which the *Sharia'a* is derived, are further explained and translated into practice by the *Sunnah* of the Prophet. *Sunnah* literally means a way, practice, rule of life; it refers to the exemplary conduct or the model behaviour of the Prophet in what he said, did or approved. Thus it became a very important source of the *Sharia'a*, only second in authority after the Holy *Qur'an*.

Besides the *Qur'an* and the *Sunnah*, the consensus of the opinion of the learned men and jurists, known in the

Sharia'a terminology as *Ijma*, plays an important role in Islamic law since it provides a broad vehicle of progress and reconstruction. *Qiyas* or analogical deduction is also recognised as one of the sources of Islamic legal system since it gives an instrument to cope with the growing needs and requirements of society. Such analogical deduction is based on very strict, logical and systematic principles. Alongside these four sources, the *Sharia'a* takes into consideration *Istihsan* or juristic preference or equity of a jurist as against *Qiyas* which helps in providing elasticity and adaptability to the entire Islamic legal system. The concept of *al-Masalih al Mursalah* (the matters which are in public interest and which are not specifically defined in the *Sharia'a*) has also become a part of the *Sharia'a* system.

What Is the Qur'an?

Answer

The *Qur'an* is believed to be the miracle of Mohammed, the proof of his prophethood and a testimony to its divine origin.

Being the verbal noun of the root word *qara'a* (to read), *Qur'an* literally means 'reading' or 'recitation'. It may be defined as 'the book containing the speech of God revealed to the Prophet Mohammed in Arabic and transmitted to us by continuous testimony'. It is a proof of the prophecy of Mohammed, the most authoritative guide for Muslims, and the first source of the *Sharia'a*. The *Ulema* are unanimous on this, and some even say that it is the only source and that all other sources are explanatory to the *Qur'an*. The salient attributes of the *Qur'an* that are indicated in this definition are five: it was revealed exclusively to the Prophet Mohammed; it was put into writing; it is all *mutawatir* (universally accurately reported); it is the inimitable speech of God; and it is recited in *salah*.

The first revelation of the *Qur'an* began on the 15th night of the month of Ramadan in the 41st year of the Prophet's life. Its first *Sura* (Chapter) was revealed in the Cave of Hira when the verse, *Recite in the name of thy Lord and Cherished who created man our of a (mere) clot of congealed blood. Proclaim and thy Lord is Most Bountiful* was revealed.

The *Qur'an* was revealed to mankind gradually, in about 23 years, through the mediation of the archangel Gabriel.

There are 114 *Suras* (chapters) and 6,235 *ayat* (verses) of unequal length in the *Qur'an*. The shortest of the *Suras* consist of 4 and the longest 286 *ayat*. Each chapter has a separate title. The longest *Suras* appear first and the *Suras* become shorter as the text proceeds. Both the order of the *ayat* within each *Sura* and the sequence of the *Suras* were re-arranged and finally determined by the Prophet in the year of his demise.

The *Qur'an* consists of manifest revelation, which is defined as communication from God to the Prophet Mohammed, conveyed by the angel Gabriel, in the very words of God. This the Prophet received in a state of wakefulness, and thus no part of the *Qur'an* originated in internal inspiration or dreams. God inspired the Prophet and the latter conveyed the concepts in his own words. All the sayings, or *Hadith*, of the Prophet fail into the category of internal revelation and, as such, are not included in the *Qur'an*.

The '*Ulema*' (religious scholars) are in agreement that the entire text of the *Qur'an* is *mutawatir*, that is, its authenticity is proven by universally accepted testimony. It has been retained both in memory and as a written record throughout the generations.

During the lifetime of the Prophet, the text of the *Qur'an* was preserved not only in memories but also in inscriptions on such available material as flat stones, wood and bones, which would explain why it could not have been compiled in a bound volume. Initially, the first Caliph, Abu Bakr, collected the *Qur'an* soon after the battle of Yamamah, which led to the death of at least 70 of the memorisers of the *Qur'an*. Zayd ibn Thabit, the scribe of the Prophet, was employed in the task of compiling the text, which he accomplished between 11 and 14 AH. But several versions and reading of this edition soon crept into use. Hence the third Caliph, 'Uthman, once again utilised the services of Zayd to verify the accuracy of the text and compiled it in a single volume. All the remaining variations were then destroyed. As a result, only one authentic text has remained in use to this day.

Out of over 6,200 *ayat*, less than one-tenth relate to law and jurisprudence, while the remainder are largely concerned with matters of belief and morality, the five pillars of the faith and a variety of other themes. Its ideas of economic and social justice, including its legal contents, are, on the whole, subsidiary to its religious call.

What Is the Sunnah?

Answer
Literally, *Sunnah* means a clear path or a beaten track but it is also used to imply normative practice, or an established course of conduct.

In pre-Islamic Arabia, the Arabs used the word *Sunnah* in reference to the ancient and continuous practices of the community that they inherited from their forefathers.

In the *Qur'an*, the word *Sunnah* has been used to imply an established practice or course of conduct.

The prime source of the religion of Islam is the *Qur'an*. The *Qur'an* is the word of Allah to all Muslims. The Prophet did not have anything to do with its words; it was revealed to him as it is now read. Whilst the *Qur'an* gives the Muslims a primary rule of life, there are many matters where guidance for practical living is necessary but about which the *Qur'an* says nothing. In such cases the obvious thing was to follow the custom or usage of the Prophet (i.e. *Sunnah*). There were ancient customs which could be accepted in some matters, but on matters peculiar to the religion of Islam there was the custom of the earliest believers who had been the contemporaries and companions of the Prophet and who presumably would act in matters of religion according to the custom of the Prophet himself. Eventually, there came into existence statements as to what the *Sunnah* of the earliest Muslims was on a variety of matters. Literally, *Sunnah* means a way or rule or manner of acting or mode of life. In consequence of this, there arose in Islam a class of students who made it their business to investigate and hand down the minutest details concerning the life of the Prophet.

After his death, reports of the Prophet's sayings and doings began to circulate. These sayings continued to increase from time to time as they were collected from the *Sahaba*, the Companions of the Prophet, and became subject to standardisation and selection.

The records of the sayings, therefore, were called *Hadith;* the rest, as a whole, was called *Sunnah* (custom or usage).

The *Hadith* is the second pillar after the *Qur'an* upon which every Muslim rests the fabric of his faith and life. The body of traditions circulated orally for some time, as indicated by the word *Hadith*, commonly used for tradition and which literally means a saying conveyed to man either through hearing or through witnessing an event. It is also used to denote 'conversation' i.e. the telling of something new.

To the *Ulema* of *Hadith, Sunnah* refers to all that is narrated from the Prophet, his acts, his sayings and whatever he has tacitly approved, plus all the reports which describe his physical attributes and character.

Notwithstanding the fact that the *Ulema* have used *Sunnah* and *Hadith* almost interchangeably, the two terms have meanings of their own. Literally, *Hadith* means a narrative, communication or news consisting of the factual account of an event. The word occurs frequently in the *Qur'an* (23 times) and in all cases it carries the meaning of a narrative or communication. In none of these instances has *Hadith* been used in its technical, exclusive sense, that is, the sayings of the Prophet. In the early days of Islam, following the demise of the Prophet, stories relating to the life and activities of the Prophet dominated all other kinds of narratives, so the word began to be used almost exclusively for a narrative from, or a saying of, the Prophet.

Hadith differs from *Sunnah* in that *Hadith* is a narration of the conduct of the Prophet whereas *Sunnah* is the example or the law that is deduced from it. *Hadith* in this sense is the vehicle or the carrier of *Sunnah*, although *Sunnah* is a wider concept and used to be so, especially before its literal meaning gave way to its juristic usage. *Sunnah* thus refers not only to the *Hadith* of the Prophet but also to the established practice of the community.

What Is the Difference between the Qur'an and the Sunnah?

Answer

The *Qur'an* was recorded in writing from beginning to end during the lifetime of the Prophet, who ascertained that the *Qur'an* was preserved as he received it through divine revelation. The Prophet clearly expressed the concern that nothing of his own *Sunnah* should be confused with the text of the *Qur'an*. This was, in fact, the main reason why he discouraged his Companions, at least at the early stage of his mission, from reducing the *Sunnah* into writing lest it be confused with the *Qur'an*. The *Sunnah*, on the other hand, was mainly retained in memory by the Companions who did not, on the whole, keep a written record of the teachings of the Prophet. There were perhaps some exceptions as the relevant literature suggests that some, though only a small number, of the Companions held collections of the *Hadith* of the Prophet which they wrote and kept in their private collections. The overall impression, however, is that this was done on a fairly limited scale.

As the *Sunnah* is the second source of the *Sharia'a* after the *Qur'an*, the *mujtahid* (Scholar of Islamic law) is bound to observe the order of priority between the *Qur'an* and *Sunnah*. Hence in his search for a solution to a particular problem, the jurist must resort to the *Sunnah* only when he fails to find any guidance in the *Qur'an*. Should there be a clear text in the *Qur'an*, it must be followed and be given priority over any ruling of the *Sunnah* which may happen to be in conflict with the *Qur'an*. The priority of the *Qur'an* over the *Sunnah* is partly a result of the fact that the *Qur'an* consists wholly of manifest revelation whereas the *Sunnah* mainly consists of internal revelation and is largely transmitted in the words of the narrators themselves. The other reason for this order of priority relates to the question of authenticity. The authenticity of the *Qur'an* is not open to doubt. It is, in other words, decisive, in respect of authenticity and must therefore take priority over the *Sunnah*.

What Is Ijma (Consensus)?

Answer

The primary sources of the *Sharia'a* are the *Qur'an* and the *Sunnah*. The secondary sources are *Ijma, Qiyas* and *Ijtihad* – which are derived from the legal injunctions of the Holy *Qur'an* and the *Sunnah* of the Prophet. The final sanction for all intellectual activities in respect of the development of *Sharia'a* comes from nowhere else but the *Qur'an*. Any *Hadith* which goes contrary to the *Qur'an* is not to be considered as authentic.

Apart from the *Qur'an* and the *Sunnah*, the two primary sources of the *Sharia'a*, there are two secondary sources *Ijma* and *Qiyas*. *Ijma* refers to the consensus of Juristic opinions of the learned *'Ulema* of the *Ummah* after the death of the Messenger of Allah, the Prophet Mohammed.

Ijma can be defined as the consensus of opinion of the companions of the Prophet *(Sahaba)* and the agreement reached on the decisions taken by the learned *Muftis'*, or jurists, on various Islamic matters.

Unlike the *Qur'an* and *Sunnah*, *Ijma* does not directly partake of divine revelation. *Ijma* is the verbal noun of the Arabic word *ajma'a*, which means to determine and to agree upon something. The second meaning of *Ijma* often subsumes the first, in that whenever there is a unanimous agreement on something, there is also a decision on that matter. Whereas a decision can be made by one individual or by many, unanimous agreement can only be reached by a plurality of individuals.

Ijma is defined as the unanimous agreement of the Muslim community for any period, following the demise of the Prophet Mohammed, on any matter.

It is clear from its definition that *Ijma* can only occur after the demise of the Prophet. During his lifetime, the Prophet alone was the highest authority on *Sharia'a*, hence the agreement or disagreement of others did not affect the overriding authority of the Prophet. In all probability, *Ijma* occurred for the first time among the Companions in the city of Medina. Following the demise of the Prophet, the Companions used to consult each other about the problems they encountered, and their collective agreement was accepted by the community. After the Companions, this leadership role passed on to the next generation, the Successors, and then to the second generation of Successors. When these latter differed on a point, they naturally referred to the views and practices of the Companions and the Successors. In this way, a fertile ground was created for the development of the theory of *Ijma*.

The essence of *Ijma* lies in the natural growth of ideas. It begins with the personal opinion of individual jurists and culminates in the universal acceptance of a particular opinion over a period of time. Differences of opinion are tolerated until a consensus emerges.

Ijma represents authority. Once an *Ijma* is established it tends to become an authority in its own right.

What Is Qiyas?

Answer

Literally, *Qiyas* means measuring or ascertaining the length, weight or quality of something.

Qiyas also means comparison, with a view to suggesting equality or similarity between two things.

Qiyas thus suggests an equality or close similarity between two things, one of which is taken as the criterion for evaluating the other.

Technically, *Qiyas* is the extension of a position from the *Sharia'a* to a new case, on the grounds that the latter has the same effective cause as the former. The original case is regulated by a given text, and *Qiyas* seeks to extend the same textual ruling to the new case. It is by virtue of the commonality of the effective cause, or *'illah*, between the original case and the new case that the application of *Qiyas* is justified. A recourse to analogy is only warranted if the solution of a new case cannot be found in the *Qur'an*, the *Sunnah* or a definite *Ijma*.

Qiyas is defined, in Islamic theological parlance, as analogy, or analogical deduction. In other words, *Qiyas* is the legal principle introduced in order to derive a logical conclusion of a certain law on a certain issue that has to do with the welfare of Muslims. However, it must be based on the *Qur'an*, *Sunnah* and *Ijma*.

This legal principle was introduced by Imam Abu Hanifah, the founder of the Hanafi school, in Iraq. The reason why he introduced it was to curb the excessive thinking and digression of the people from strict Islamic principles.

During the period of the Abbasids, people engaged themselves in reading various textbooks on logic philosophy, etymology, linguistics, literatures of various places, and foreign textbooks, which, some argued, tended to corrupt their minds and lead them astray. They wanted to apply what they had studied in these foreign text books to Islamic jurisprudence. Many new Muslims in faraway lands had brought, with their philosophical outlook, their culture and even some religious notions in the fold of Islam. Abu Hanifah introduced *Qiyas so* as to curb their excessive thinking and to ensure that Islamic principles were upheld.

During the lifetime of the Companions of the Prophet the Companions arrived at various decisions on analogical deductions. To take an example concerning the punishment that should be given to a drunkard, Sayyidna Ali concluded by saying, 'He who drinks, get drunk; he who gets drunk, raves; he who raves, accuses people falsely and he who accuses people falsely should be given eighty strokes of cane. Therefore, he who drinks should be given eighty strokes of cane.' There is nothing wrong in using *Qiyas* in deriving a logical conclusion in Islamic law in as much as that conclusion does not go against the injunctions of the Holy *Qur'an* or the *Sunnah* of the Prophet.

What Is an Islamic Bank?

Answer

Islamic financial institutions are those that are based, in their objectives and operations, on Qur'anic principles. They are thus set apart from 'conventional' institutions, which have no such religious preoccupations. Islamic banks provide commercial services which comply with the religious injunctions of Islam. Islamic banks provide services to their customers free of interest (the Arabic term for which is *riba*), and the giving and taking of interest is prohibited in all transactions. This prohibition makes an Islamic banking system differ fundamentally from a conventional banking system.

What Is Riba?

Answer

Technically, *riba* refers to the addition in the amount of the principal of a loan according to the time for which it is loaned and the amount of the loan. In earlier historical times there was a fierce debate as to whether *riba* relates to interest or usury, although there now appears to be a consensus of opinion among Islamic scholars that the term extends to all forms of interest.

The term *riba*, in Islamic law (the *Sharia'a*), means an addition, however slight, over and above the principal. According to the Federal *Sharia'a* Court of Pakistan, this means that the concept covers both usury and interest; that it applies to all forms of interest, whether large or small, simple or compound, doubled or redoubled; and that the Islamic injunction is not only against exorbitant or excessive interest, but also against even a minimal rate of interest. Financial systems based on Islamic tenets are therefore dedicated to the elimination of the payment and receipt of interest in all forms. It is this taboo that makes Islamic banks and other financial institutions different, in principle, from their Western conventional counterparts.

There are a range of modern interpretations of why *riba* is considered *haram* (forbidden) but these are strictly secondary to the religious underpinnings. These are discussed further in Chapter 3.

If Islamic Banks Cannot Charge Interest How Can They Make Money?

Answer

This rejection of using interest poses the central question of what replaces the interest rate mechanism in an Islamic framework. Financial intermediation is at the heart of modern financial systems. If the paying and receiving of interest is prohibited, how do Islamic banks operate? Here profit and loss sharing (PLS) comes in, substituting PLS for interest as a method of resource allocation and financial intermediation.

The basic idea underlying Islamic banking can be stated simply. The operations of Islamic financial institutions primarily are based on a PLS principle. An Islamic bank does not charge interest but rather participates in the yield resulting from the use of funds. The depositors also share in the profits of the bank according to a predetermined ratio. There is thus a partnership between the Islamic bank and its depositors, on one side, and between the bank and its investment clients, on the other side, as a manager of depositors' resources in productive uses. This is in contrast with a conventional bank, which mainly borrows funds paying interest on one side of the balance sheet and lends funds, charging interest, on the other. The complexity of Islamic banking comes from the variety (and nomenclature) of the instruments employed, and in understanding the underpinnings of Islamic law. PLS is discussed in more detail later in the text.

What Are the Six Key Principal Activities of Islamic Banks?

Answer

Six key principles drive the activities of Islamic banks. These are as follows:

1. the prohibition of predetermined loan repayments as interest *(riba)*;
2. PLS is at the heart of the Islamic system;
3. making money out of money is unacceptable. All financial transactions must be asset-backed;
4. prohibition of speculative behaviour;
5. only *Sharia'a* approved contracts are acceptable;
6. the sanctity of contracts.

What Does 'Predetermined Payments Are Prohibited' Mean?

Answer

Any predetermined payment over and above the actual amount of principal is prohibited. Islam allows only one kind of loan and that is *qard al hassan* (literally 'good loan') whereby the lender does not charge any interest or additional amount over the money lent. Traditional Muslim jurists have construed this principle so strictly that, according to one Islamic scholar, 'the prohibition applies to any advantage or benefits that the lender might secure out of the *qard* (loan) such as riding the borrower's mule, eating at his table, or even taking advantage of the shade of his wall'. The principle derived from the quotation emphasises that any associated or indirect benefits which could potentially accrue to the lender are also prohibited.

What Does Profit and Loss Sharing Mean?

Answer

The principle here is that the lender must share in the profits or losses arising out of the enterprise for which the money was lent. Islam encourages Muslims to invest their money and to become partners in order to share profits and risks in the business, instead of becoming creditors. Islamic finance is based on the belief that the provider of capital and the user of capital should equally share the risk of business ventures, whether these are manufacturing industries, service companies or simple trade deals. Translated into banking terms, the depositor, the bank and the borrower should all share the risks and the rewards of financing business ventures.

This is unlike the interest-based commercial banking system, where all the pressure is on the borrower; he must pay back his loan, with the agreed interest, regardless of the success or failure of his venture.

The principle, which thereby emerges, is that in order to try and ensure that investments are made into productive enterprises Islam encourages these types of investments in order that the community may ultimately benefit. However, Islam is not willing to allow a loophole to exist for those who do not wish to invest and take risks but are rather intent on hoarding money or depositing money in a bank in return for receiving interest (*riba*) on these funds for no risk (other than the bank becoming insolvent).

Accordingly, under Islam, either people invest with risk or suffer loss by keeping their money idle. Islam encourages the notion of higher risks and higher returns and promotes it by leaving no other avenue available to investors, the objective here being that high-risk investments provide a stimulus to the economy and encourages entrepreneurs to maximise their efforts to make them succeed, with appropriate benefits to the community.

What Does Risk-Sharing Mean?

Answer

One of the most important features of Islamic banking is that it promotes risk-sharing between the providers of funds (investors) and the user of funds (entrepreneurs). By contrast, under conventional banking, the investor is assured of a predetermined rate of interest.

In conventional banking, all the risk is borne by the entrepreneur. Whether the project succeeds and produces a profit or fails and produces a loss, the owner of capital is still rewarded with a predetermined return. In Islam, this kind of unjust distribution is not allowed. In pure Islamic banking, both the investor and the entrepreneur share the results of the project in an equitable way. In the case of profit, both share this in pre-agreed proportions. In the case of loss, all financial loss is borne by the capital supplier with the entrepreneur being penalised by receiving no return (wages or salary) for his endeavours.

Under conventional banking, almost all that matters to a bank is that its loan and the interest thereon are paid on time. Therefore, in granting loans, the dominant consideration is the credit worthiness of the borrower. Under PLS banking, the bank will receive a return only if the project succeeds and produces a profit. Therefore, it is reasoned, an Islamic bank will be more concerned with the soundness of the project and the business acumen and managerial competence of the entrepreneur.

What Does 'Making Money Out of Money Is Not Acceptable' Mean?

Answer

Making money from money is not Islamically acceptable.
Money, in Islam, is only a medium of exchange, a way of
defining the value of a thing. It has no value in itself, and
therefore should not be allowed to generate more money, via
fixed interest payments, simply by being put in a bank or lent
to someone else.

The human effort, initiative and risk involved in a productive
venture are more important than the money used to finance
it. Muslim jurists consider money as potential capital rather
than capital, meaning that money becomes capital only when
it is invested in business. Accordingly, money advanced to a
business as a loan is regarded as a debt of the business and
not capital and, as such, it is not entitled to any return (i.e.
interest).

Muslims are encouraged to spend and/or invest in productive
investments and are discouraged from keeping money idle.
Hoarding money is regarded as being Islamically unacceptable. In Islam, money represents purchasing power, which is
considered to be the only proper use of money. This purchasing power (money) cannot be used to make more purchasing
power (money) without undergoing the intermediate step of
it being used for the purchase of goods and services.

What Does 'Uncertainty Is Prohibited' Mean?

Answer

Gharar (uncertainty, risk or speculation) is also prohibited.

Under this prohibition, any transaction entered into should be free from uncertainty, risk and speculation. Contracting parties should have perfect knowledge of the counter values (goods received and/or prices paid) intended to be exchanged as a result of their transactions. Also, parties cannot predetermine a guaranteed profit. This is based on the principle of 'uncertain gains' which, on a strict interpretation, does not even allow an undertaking from the customer to repay the borrowed principal plus an amount designed to take inflation into account. The rationale behind the prohibition is the wish to protect the weak from exploitation. Therefore, options and futures are considered as un-Islamic and so are forward foreign exchange transactions, given that forward exchange rates are determined by interest rate differentials, in other words *riba* based transactions.

What Does 'Only Sharia'a Approved Contracts Are Acceptable' Mean?

Answer

Conventional banking is secular in its orientation. In contrast, in the Islamic system, all economic agents have to work within the moral value system of Islam. Islamic banks are no exception. As such, they cannot finance any project which conflicts with the moral value system of Islam. For example, Islamic banks are not allowed to finance a distillery, a casino, a night club or any other activity which is prohibited by Islam or is *known* to be harmful to society.

What Does Sanctity of Contracts Mean?

Answer

Many verses in the Holy *Qur'an* encourage trade and commerce, and the attitude of Islam is that there should be no impediment to honest and legitimate trade and business. It is a duty for Muslims to earn a living, support their families and give charity to those less fortunate.

Just as Islam regulates and influences all other spheres of life, so it also governs the conduct of business and commerce. Muslims have a moral obligation to conduct their business activities in accordance with the requirements of their religion. They should be fair, honest and just towards others. A special obligation exists upon vendors as there is no doctrine of *caveat emptor* in Islam. Monopolies and price-fixing are prohibited.

The basic principles of commercial *Sharia'a* law are laid down in the four root transactions of (1) sales (*bay*), transfer of the ownership or corpus of property for a consideration; (2) hire (*Ijara*), transfer of the usufruct (right to use) of property for a consideration; (3) gift (*hiba*), gratuitous transfer of the corpus of property and (4) loan (*ariyah*), gratuitous transfer of the usufruct of property.

These basic principles are then applied to the various specific transactions of, for example, pledge, deposit, guarantee, agency, assignment, land tenancy, *Waqf* foundations (religious or charitable bodies) and partnerships.

Islam upholds contractual obligations and the disclosure of information as a sacred duty. This feature is intended to reduce the risk of asymmetric information and moral hazard.

What Is Takaful?

Answer

Takaful means 'guaranteeing each other' and is based on the principles of *Ta'awun* (mutual co-operation) and *Tabarru* (donation), where a group of *Takaful* participants (policyholders) agree between themselves to share the risk of a potential loss to any of them, by making a donation of all or part of their *Takaful* contribution (premium) to compensate for a loss.

In conventional insurance the risk is transferred from the policyholder to the insurance company which brings the elements of uncertainty and chance in the contract as one of the two parties makes a loss. *Takaful* is a structure in which the risk is shared between all participants, removing the elements of uncertainty and gambling from the contract.

How Does Takaful Work?

Answer

The participants of *Takaful* each pay a *Takaful* contribution, based on their individual risk and the likelihood of making a claim, to create a *Takaful* fund. The nature of the risk covered and the period of cover are specified in the *Takaful* contract (insurance policy).

The *Takaful* fund is invested strictly in *Halal* activities under non-interest-bearing conditions in order to maximise the fund value in a *Sharia'a*-compliant manner.

If it is ascertained that the *Takaful* fund is over-funded; the amount by which the *Takaful* fund is over-funded will be distributed to eligible *Takaful* participants by way of a participation discount (in addition to any No Claim Discount) from participants of next year's *Takaful* contribution.

Is the Concept of Insurance Haram in Islam?

Answer

The concept of insurance is not *haram* in Islam when undertaken in the framework of *Takaful* or mutual co-operation and solidarity. Contrary to conventional insurance, *Takaful* does not contain non-permissible elements such as *gharar* (uncertainty), gambling and investing in interest-bearing instruments.

Why Is Conventional Insurance Considered Haram for Muslims?

Answer

Conventional insurance is based on a contract of exchange (sale) between the insurance company and the insured person. This contract is void because it has one or all of the following elements, which are not permissible from a *Sharia'a* perspective:

Gharar (uncertainties): Conventional insurance has an element of *gharar* due to the promise to pay a sum of money upon the occurrence of unexpected events.

Maisir (gambling): Existence of *gharar* (uncertainties) leads to *Maisir* (gambling) in conventional insurance. The insured may either lose all the premiums he has paid or be compensated for the losses he incurs for the insured event.

Riba (usury/interest): The investments of insurance funds in interest-bearing securities such as bonds and stocks which do not comply with *Sharia'a* principles poses a major problem for Muslims who purchase conventional insurance.

Why Do Muslims Need Takaful If Everything That Happens in This World Is by the Will of Allah (Qada' and Qadar)?

Answer

The taking out of a *Takaful* policy is not to supersede the power or will of Allah in one's life, death or destiny (*Qada'* and *Qadar*) but to achieve the pleasure of Allah who orders Muslims to 'help . . . one another in righteousness and piety.' The main objective of *Takaful* is to provide a level of comfort to the participants against unexpected future risk through mutual co-operation.

Is Takaful Sharia'a Compliant?

Answer

Takaful is *Sharia'a* compliant given that it is based on the principle of co-operation, not sale or exchange, and mitigates the objectionable aspects of *gharar*, *Maisir* and *riba*. This is contrary to conventional insurance, where policyholders pay premiums as a price for protection against a catastrophe. If a catastrophe occurs, the policyholder will be protected. The policyholder will lose the premium to the insurance company if such a catastrophe does not occur.

In contrast, a contribution to a *Takaful* fund is an agreement with other members (participants) of the fund to mutually help each other by way of providing financial assistance should any member of the fund suffer a catastrophe or disaster. Moreover, a *Takaful* fund invests the contributions in a *Sharia'a*-compliant manner, avoiding any interest-based instruments. In addition, any surplus will be redistributed to the participants.

The *Takaful* company therefore only manages this pool (for a fee) for the benefit of the members/participants.

What Is the Ta'awun Model?

Answer

The *Ta'awun* model (co-operative insurance) practices the concept of *Mudaraba* in daily transactions, where it encourages the Islamic values of brotherhood, unity, solidarity and mutual co-operation. In the *Mudaraba* model the *Takaful* company and the participant share the direct investment income, while the participant is entitled to 100% of the surplus, with no deduction made prior to the distribution.

What Are the Differences between Takaful and Conventional Insurance?

Answer

The major differences can be summarised as below:

	Takaful	**Conventional insurance**
Contract	The contract among participants of the *Takaful* fund is the contract of *Tabarru* (donation, gift) and therefore is about co-operation and mutual help amongst them. *Takaful* contracts are very transparent	This is a contract of exchange, that is, a sale and purchase agreement between the insurer (the company) and the insured upon which the insured buys and the insurer sells the policy
Responsibility for providing protection	Participants are responsible for protecting each other through *Tabarru* (donation, gift). The *Takaful* operator only manages the *Takaful* operations on behalf of participants	Non-*Takaful* companies, other than mutual companies, provide protection in return for premiums. Policyholders have no relationship amongst themselves though they contribute to the same insurance fund

	Takaful	**Conventional insurance**
Surplus	The *Takaful* surplus belongs to the participants. A portion of the surplus is to be distributed back to the participants	Any surplus belongs to the insurer
Liability of the insurer/ operator	The *Takaful* operator, acting on behalf of the participants, pays claims from the *Takaful* fund	The insurer is responsible for paying claims from its assets (insurance funds and shareholders' fund)
Investment	All funds are invested in *Sharia'a*-compliant investments	Funds received may be invested in both *Sharia'a* and non-*Sharia'a* investments

How Does the Mudaraba Takaful Model Work?

Answer

This is a PLS model. The participant and the *Takaful* insurer share the surplus. The sharing of such profit (surplus) differs on the basis of a ratio mutually agreed upon between the contracting parties. Generally, these risk-sharing arrangements allow the *Takaful* insurer to share in the underwriting results from operations, as well as any favourable performance returns on invested premiums.

How Does the Wakala Takaful Model Work?

Answer

This is a fee-based model. Co-operative risk-sharing occurs among participants where a *Takaful* insurer simply earns a fee for services (as a *Wakeel*, or 'Agent') and does not participate or share in any underwriting outcomes. The insurer's fee may include a fund management fee and a performance incentive fee.

How Does the Waqf Takaful Model Work?

Answer

Unlike the *Mudaraba* and *Wakala* models, *Waqf* operates as a social/governmental enterprise, and programmes are operated on a non-profit basis. Under the *Waqf* model, any surplus or profit is not owned directly by either the insurer or the participants, and there is no mechanism to distribute any surplus funds. In effect, the insurer retains the surplus funds to support the participant community.

What Are the Two Separate Funds in Takaful?

Answer

Firstly, there is a *Takaful* (or policyholders') fund and secondly, there is an operator's (or shareholders') fund. The *Takaful* fund operates under pure co-operative principles in a way similar to conventional mutual insurance entities. Underwriting deficits and surpluses are accrued over time within this fund, to which the operator has no direct recourse.

As a result, the *Takaful* fund is effectively ring-fenced and protected from the default of the operator's fund. Management expenses and seed capital are borne by the operator's fund, where the main income takes the form of either a predefined management fee (to cover costs) or a share of investment returns and underwriting results (or a combination of both).

What Is Family Takaful?

Answer

Family *Takaful* provides members with protection and long-term savings. Members, or their beneficiaries, will be provided with financial benefits if they suffer a tragedy. At the same time, they will enjoy long-term personal savings because part of their contribution will be deposited in an account for the purpose of savings. Members will be able to enjoy investment returns from the savings portion based on a pre-agreed ratio.

How Does Family Takaful Work?

Answer

When members participate in family *Takaful*, they will contribute a certain amount of money to a *Takaful* fund. They will undertake a contract (*aqd*) for part of their contribution to be in the form of a participative contribution (*Tabarru'*) and the other part for savings and investment.

The contribution in the form of *Tabarru'* will be placed in a fund (participants' special account [PSA]) that will be used to fulfil any obligation of mutual help, should any of the participants face misfortune arising from death or permanent disability. If members survive until the date of maturity of the plan, they will be entitled to share the net surplus from the fund, if any.

The *Takaful* operator will invest the savings and investment contribution (participant's account [PA]), and the profit will be shared between the member and the *Takaful* operator according to a pre-agreed ratio.

What Is General Takaful?

Answer
This is to cover everyday risks including the following:

- *Motor insurance*
  Cars, motorcycles, taxis, commercial vehicles and vans, industrial and agricultural vehicles.

- *Building insurance*
  Residential properties including houses, flats and holiday homes, commercial properties including offices, shops and factories and community buildings including mosques and schools.

- *Contents insurance*
  Household contents, personal effects and valuables.

- *Business insurance*
  Business premises – fire and theft, and so on., stock, equipment and materials, employer's liability, public liability, loss of revenue, professional indemnity, import/export and the transportation of goods.

What Are Sukuk?

Answer

The term *Sukuk* is the Arabic plural of *Sakk* which means a 'legal instrument, deed, cheque.' *Sukuk* are financial certificates but can be seen as the Islamic equivalent of a bond. However, fixed income and interest-bearing bonds are not permissible in Islam; hence *Sukuk* are securities that comply with *Sharia'a* law and its investment principles.

These principles prohibit the charging, or paying of interest.

Sukuk are securitised assets and therefore belong to the category of asset-backed securities (ABS). Unlike conventional bond structures, *Sukuk* need to have an underlying tangible asset transaction either in ownership or in a master lease agreement.

Generally, *Sukuk* are a form of commercial paper that provides an investor with ownership in an underlying asset. It is an ABS that is *Sharia'a* compliant.

The *Taskeek* model for *Sukuk* securitisation is derived from the conventional securitisation process in which a special purpose vehicle (SPV) is set up to acquire assets and to issue financial claims on the assets. These financial asset claims represent a proportionate beneficial ownership to the *Sukuk* holders.

What Do Sukuk Represent?

Answer

Sukuk represent an undivided proportionate ownership interest in an asset with the corresponding right to the Islamically acceptable income streams generated by the asset.

Sukuk have economic characteristics similar to those of a conventional bond, but are structured so as to be compliant with *Sharia'a* law and can be sold to Islamic investors who are prohibited, by *Sharia'a* law, from investing in conventional debt securities.

Sukuk, sometimes referred to as Islamic bonds, are better described as Islamic investment certificates. This distinction is as crucial as it is important. The distinction is important as a bond is a contractual obligation whereby the issuer is obliged to pay bond holders, on certain specified dates, interest and principal.

In comparison, under a *Sukuk* structure, the *Sukuk* holders each hold an undivided beneficial ownership in the underlying assets. Consequently, *Sukuk* holders are entitled to share the revenue generated by the *Sukuk* assets as well as being entitled to share the proceeds of the realisation of the *Sukuk* assets.

Why Have Islamic Bonds?

Answer

Conventional bonds that yield interest, or *riba*, are prohibited under *Sharia'a* law.

Furthermore, those who buy and sell conventional bonds are rarely interested in what is actually being financed through the bond issue. This could include activities and industries that are deemed *haram*, such as the production or sale of alcohol.

A number of *Sharia'a* scholars, most notably Mohammed Taqi Usmani, have stressed that one of the distinguishing features legitimising Islamic finance is that it must involve the funding of trade in, or the production of, real assets. Merely funding the purchase of financial securities would involve second-order financing akin to derivatives-related activities, the subsequent gearing being speculative and involving uncertainty, or *gharar*.

As Islamic finance is by nature participatory, purchasers of *Sukuk* securities have the right to be given information on the purposes for which their monies are to be allocated. In other words, the funding raised through Islamic bond issues should be hypothecated or earmarked rather than used for general unspecified purposes, whether by a sovereign or corporate issuer. This implies that identifiable assets should back the *Sukuk*.

What Are the Essential Underlying Concepts of Sukuk?

Answer

- Transparency and clarity of rights and obligations.
- Income from the securities must be related to the purpose for which the funding is used, and not simply comprise interest.
- Securities should be backed by real underlying assets, rather than being simply paper derivatives.
- They are tradable *Sharia'a*-compliant capital market products providing medium- to long-term fixed or variable rates of return.
- The credit quality of *Sukuk* instruments is assessed and rated by international rating agencies, which investors use as a guideline to assess risk/return parameters of *Sukuk* issues.
- They are characterised by regular periodic income streams during the investment period with easy and efficient settlement and also provide the possibility of capital appreciation.
- The existence of a secondary market provides liquidity to the *Sukuk* instruments.

What Is the Islamic Legitimacy of Sukuk?

Answer

At the request of delegates from Jordan, Pakistan and Malaysia, the Academy of the Organization of the Islamic Conference, based in Saudi Arabia, considered the question of Islamic investment certificates at their fourth annual plenary session, held in Jeddah in February 1988.

The scholars noted that the *Sharia'a* encourages the documentation of contracts as stipulated in *Sura* 2:282 of the *Qur'an*:

> When ye deal with each other, in transactions involving future obligations in a fixed period of time, reduce them to writing … It is more just in the sight of God, more suitable as evidence and more convenient to prevent doubts among yourselves.

Subject to proper legal documentation, the Fiqh Academy, under decision number 5 of 1988 ruled that:

- any collection of assets can be represented in a written note or bond;
- this bond or note can be sold at a market price provided that the composition of the group of assets, represented by the security, consists of a majority of physical assets and financial rights, with only a minority being cash and interpersonal debts.

Although there is no compulsion to comply with the rulings of the Fiqh Academy, their rulings carry considerable weight with most Islamic financial institutions and also with their *Sharia'a* committees and advisers.

What Are Ijara Sukuk?

Answer

These are *Sukuk* that are based on the *Ijara* mode of finance. They are one of the most common *Sukuk* issuance types, especially for leasing and project finance. *Ijara Sukuk* involve a leasing structure sometimes coupled with a right available to the lessee to purchase the asset at the end of the lease period (finance lease). The certificates are issued on stand-alone assets identified on the balance sheet.

The rental rates of return on those *Sukuk* can be fixed or floating, depending on the agreement. The cash flow from the lease including rental payments and principal repayments are passed through to investors in the form of coupon and principal payments. *Ijara Sukuk* provide an efficient medium- to long-term mode of financing.

These instruments have been used in a variety of cross-border applications for an increasing range of asset classes including ships, aircraft, telecommunications equipment and power station turbines.

What Are Istisna'a Sukuk?

Answer

These are *Sukuk* that are based on the *Istisna'a* mode of finance. *Istisna'a* is a mode of finance involving construction and manufacturing. This type of *Sukuk* has been used for the advance funding of real estate development, major industrial projects or large items of equipment such as turbines, power plants, ships or aircraft.

The Islamic financial institution funds the manufacturer or the contractor during the construction of the asset, acquires title to that asset and upon completion either immediately passes title to the developer on agreed deferred payment terms or, possibly, leases the asset to the developer under an *Ijara Sukuk*. However, it should be noted that, if the *Sukuk* are listed during the *Istisna'a* period, the *Sukuk* can only be traded at par as the underlying assets do not yet exist. This is due to the *Sharia'a* ruling that debt cannot be traded, except at par value.

What Are Salam Sukuk?

Answer

These are *Sukuk* that are based on the *Salam* mode of finance. The concept of *Salam Sukuk* refers to a sale, whereby the seller undertakes to supply a specific commodity to the buyer at a future date in return for an advanced price paid in full on a spot basis. The price is in cash but the supply of the purchased good is deferred. As a form of financing, the purchaser is able to acquire the assets by advance payment at a discounted price and subsequently sells the assets upon delivery.

Salam Sukuk represent a type of a forward contract which is forbidden under *Sharia'a* law unless there are strict conditions attached that aim at the elimination of uncertainty.

Salam Sukuk differ from *Istisna'a Sukuk* in that the purchase price for the assets under *Salam Sukuk* must be paid in full and the date of delivery must be fixed.

What are Mudaraba Sukuk?

Answer

These are *Sukuk* that are based on the *Mudaraba* mode of finance. *Mudaraba* is an agreement made between one party, who provides the capital, and another party (an entrepreneur) to enable the entrepreneur to carry out business projects, which will be on a profit-sharing basis, according to predetermined ratios agreed on earlier (participation or trust financing). In the case of losses these are borne by the provider of the funds only.

What Are Musharaka Sukuk?

Answer

These are *Sukuk* that are based on the *Musharaka* mode of finance. *Musharaka* is very similar to the *Mudaraba* contract and it is widely used in equity financing. The structure of *Musharaka* requires that both parties provide financing to the projects. In the case of losses, both parties will lose in proportion to the size of their investment.

What Are Murabaha Sukuk?

Answer

These are *Sukuk* that are based on the *Murabaha* mode of finance. The *Murabaha* technique (cost-plus financing) is one of the most widely used instruments for Islamic short-term financing.

The structure of *Murabaha* is relatively straightforward and is based on a declared mark-up integrated into the selling price with a deferred payment. The Islamic financial institution purchases and takes title of the necessary equipment or goods from a third party; the Islamic financial institution then sells the equipment or goods to its customer at cost plus a reasonable profit.

What Are the AAOIFI Sukuk Classifications?

Answer

In response to the emergence of interest in issuances of Islamic asset-backed financial instruments, the Accounting and Auditing Organization for Islamic Financial Institutions (AAOIFI) released an exposure draft of its *Sharia'a standards concerning Sukuk* in November 2002. According to the exposure draft: 'Investment *Sukuk* are certificates of equal value representing, after closing subscription, receipt of the value of the certificates and putting it to use as planned, common title to shares and rights in tangible assets, usufructs, and services, or equity of a given project or equity of a special investment activity'. (*Exposure Draft of AAOIFI Sharia'a Standard No. 18*, p. 4)

AAOIFI issued standards for 14 different types of *Sukuk*, where some of these *Sukuk* are classified as tradable and others are classified as non-tradable, based on the type and characteristics of the issued *Sukuk*.

How and Why Has the Islamic Legitimacy of Sukuk Been Challenged?

Answer

Sheikh Taqi Usmani, Chairman of the AAOIFI *Sharia'a* Board commented, in late 2007, that about 85% of Islamic bonds (*Sukuk*) did not really comply with *Sharia'a* law. The whole rationale for the creation of *Sukuk* was to create an Islamically acceptable instrument that did not have the *Ribawi* (meaning linked to *riba*) elements associated with conventional bonds.

Usmani's comments paralysed the industry.

Some 160 institutions from more than 30 countries are members of AAOIFI. The AAOIFI standards are mandatory in Bahrain, the Dubai International Financial Centre, Jordan, Qatar, Sudan and Syria, and are used as guidelines elsewhere. It is important to note that AAOIFI standards are not mandatory in Malaysia.

AAOIFI has a *Sharia'a* board of 20 *Sharia'a* scholars, who are also members of the *Sharia'a* boards of most of the world's largest financial institutions – hence the industry-wide paralysis.

What Did Taqi Usmani Say?

Answer

His comments revolved around three issues:

Issue 1. 'If sukuk are to be issued for existing businesses then the sukuk must ensure that sukuk holders have complete ownership in real assets'.

What is his reasoning here?

What distinguishes *Sukuk* from conventional bonds is that they represent ownership in assets that bring profits or leased assets that bring revenues. However many *Sukuk*, he argued, have been issued in which there is some doubt as to whether they really represent ownership.

Issue 2. 'If there is to be an incentive for the sukuk manager it should be based on the profits expected from the enterprise and not on the basis of an interest rate. It is unlawful for a manager to lend money when actual profits are less than expected'.

Many *Sukuk* stipulate a return to the *Sukuk* manager based on the London inter-bank offered rate (LIBOR) under the assumption, some might say pretence, that this is an incentive for good management. However Usmani points out that any incentive should be based on the difference between expected profits and actual profits. The LIBOR link has nothing to do with measuring business efficiency and everything to do with the need to market the products.

In addition, Usmani pointed out that in the event of a short-fall, if funds are paid to *Sukuk* holders then effectively they are provided with a loan.

Either way the returns to *Sukuk* holders are not according to *Sharia'a* investment principles of risk and return, with too many *Sukuk* offering effectively fixed returns.

Issue 3. 'It is unlawful for a manager to commit to repurchase assets at face value. Instead their resale must be undertaken on the basis of the net value of the assets, or at a price that is agreed at the time of purchase'.

What is his reasoning here?

A promise to pay back capital, irrespective of the performance of the asset, violates the principle of risk- and profit sharing on which *Sukuk* should be based.

As Usmani said 'You must face the actual consequences of your investment. For current sukuk, risk is not shared and reward is not shared according to the actual venture proceeds. About 85% of sukuk are structured this way'.

Without a repurchase agreement at a set price, on maturity, the return on the *Sukuk* would depend upon the performance of the underlying asset, which may deter issuers and investors looking for the steady predictable returns of bonds. Many of the *Sukuk* investors have, in fact, been conventional investors seeking these fixed returns.

How Has the Industry Responded and What Are the Implications?

Answer

Following AAOIFI meetings in Medina, Mecca and Bahrain, a press release was issued in late February 2008 designed to clarify the *Sharia'a* status of *Sukuk*. There were five key issues.

Issue 1. 'All tradable *Sukuk* should represent holdings of the *Sukuk* holders – with all their relevant rights and obligations – in physical assets that may be legally and lawfully acquired whether in kind, usufruct or services in line with the AAOIFI *Sharia'a* Standards'.

What are the implications of this?

At face value this means that a true sale (meaning ownership of the assets must legally move) with all the SPV implications, and so on, is now the only form of acceptable *Sukuk*. If this is the case then it would have dramatic implications, particularly for Sovereign *Sukuk*. Most governments issuing *Sukuk* use strategic assets, airports, and so on, to back the *Sukuk*. They may now be reluctant to risk losing ownership of these assets.

Issue 2. 'The tradable *Sukuk* should not normally represent either payables or revenues'.

What are the implications of this?

This is presumably to exclude *Murabaha* and *Salam Sukuk* which are debt based and *haram* as only being tradable in the secondary market at face value – hence the payables comment. However, the returns payable to *Sukuk* holders are based on revenues earned from the underlying asset and should be eminently acceptable under the *Sharia'a*.

Issue 3. '*Sukuk* managers are not allowed to commit to lend *Sukuk* holders any deficits that may arise between expected and realised profits. A provision may be formed to make up such deficits as possible provided that such is stipulated in the prospectus'.

What are the implications of this?

This does not seem to deal with Usmani's criticisms. If there is a shortfall, Usmani would argue, that it should be reflected in the payout to the *Sukuk* holder in line with *Sharia'a* principles. A reserve is perfectly acceptable but where does the reserve come from? If it is from capital then investors should be told that a proportion of their investment will not go towards potential returns based on PLS. If it is based on returns then what if only losses have occurred?

Issue 4. 'The *Mudarib, Sharik* or investment agent should not undertake to buy the assets from the *Sukuk* holders at face value at maturity date. However, this undertaking may be based on the net asset value, market value, cash equivalent value or any price agreed upon at the time of purchase'.

What are the implications of this?

With regard to purchase undertakings if you have a clause which says 'for a price agreed at the time of purchase' is this not tantamount to a potential guarantee? In other words, this ruling is unclear.

Issue 5. 'The *Sharia'a* supervisory board should verify all contracts and ensure that all stages are in compliance with *Sharia'a* Standards'.

What are the implications of this?

This seems to suggest that *Sharia'a* board responsibilities are to become far more onerous regarding scrutiny than they have been in the past. This, of course, may be highly desirable. However, given the shortage of scholars this seems to potentially slow down the growth of the industry, possibly severely.

What Are the Components of the Islamic Financial Infrastructure?

Answer

At the international level the Islamic financial infrastructure includes the following:

- The Accounting and Auditing Organisation for Islamic Financial Institutions (AAOIFI), set up in 1991;
- The Islamic Financial Services Board (IFSB), set up in 2002. This was established by several central banks and monetary authorities, working together with the Islamic Development Bank (IDB), International Monetary Fund (IMF) and AAOIFI;
- The Liquidity Management Centre (LMC), established on 29 July 2002 in the Kingdom of Bahrain;
- The International Islamic Financial Market (IIFM), set up in 2002;
- The International Islamic Rating Agency (IIRA), set up in 2007;
- The Islamic Research and Training Institute (IRTI), established by the IDB in 1981;
- The General Council for Islamic Banks and Financial Institutions (GCIBFI), set up in 2001;
- The Arbitration Centre for Islamic Banks and Financial Institutions (ARCIFI), set up in 2005.

Figure 2.1 summarises these institutions.

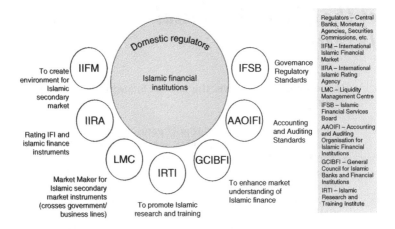

Figure 2.1: The Islamic financial infrastructure.

What Is the Accounting and Auditing Organization for Islamic Financial Institutions (AAOIFI)?

Answer

AAOIFI is an Islamic international autonomous not-for-profit corporate body that prepares accounting, auditing, governance, ethics and *Sharia'a* standards for Islamic financial institutions and the industry.

AAOIFI was established in accordance with the Agreement of Association which was signed by Islamic financial institutions on 26 February 1990 in Algiers. AAOIFI was registered on 27 March 1991, in the State of Bahrain.

As an independent international organisation, AAOIFI is supported by institutional members (as at January 2009 this includes 155 members from 40 countries, so far) including central banks, Islamic financial institutions and other participants from the international Islamic banking and finance industry.

AAOIFI has gained wide support for the implementation of its standards. These are now adopted in the Kingdom of Bahrain, Dubai International Finance Centre, Jordan, Lebanon, Qatar, Sudan and Syria. The relevant authorities in Australia, Indonesia, Malaysia, Pakistan, Kingdom of Saudi Arabia and South Africa have issued guidelines that are based on AAOIFI's standards and pronouncements.

What Are the Objectives of AAOIFI?

Answer

The objectives of AAOIFI are as follows:

1. To develop accounting and auditing concepts relevant to Islamic financial institutions
2. To disseminate accounting and auditing concepts relevant to Islamic financial institutions and its applications through training, seminars, publication of periodical newsletters, carrying out and commissioning of research and other means
3. To prepare, promulgate and interpret accounting and auditing standards for Islamic financial institutions
4. To review and amend accounting and auditing standards for Islamic financial institutions.

What Is the Islamic Financial Services Board (IFSB)?

Answer
The IFSB is an international organisation that issues guiding principles and standards within the banking, insurance and capital market sectors in order to promote stability in the Islamic financial services industry.

Background to the IFSB
The IFSB, which is based in Kuala Lumpur, Malaysia, was officially inaugurated on 3 November 2002 and started operations on 10 March 2003. It serves as an international standard-setting body of regulatory and supervisory agencies that have a vested interest in ensuring the soundness and stability of the Islamic financial services industry. This is defined broadly to include banking, capital markets and insurance. In advancing this mission, the IFSB promotes the development of a prudent and transparent Islamic financial services industry through introducing new, or adapting existing, international standards consistent with *Sharia'a* principles, and recommending them for adoption.

To this end, the work of the IFSB complements that of the Basel Committee on Banking Supervision, the International Organisation of Securities Commissions and the International Association of Insurance Supervisors.

As January 2008, 150 members of the IFSB include 37 regulatory and supervisory authorities as well as the IMF, World Bank, Bank for International Settlements, IDB, Asian Development Bank, and 108 market players and professional firms operating in 29 countries.

Malaysia, the host country of the IFSB, has enacted a law known as the IFSB Act 2002, which gives the IFSB the immunities and privileges that are usually granted to international organisations and diplomatic missions.

What Are the Objectives of the IFSB?

Answer

The objectives of the IFSB are as follows:

1. To promote the development of a prudent and transparent Islamic financial services industry through introducing new, or adapting existing, international standards consistent with *Sharia'a* principles and recommending these for adoption

2. To provide guidance on the effective supervision and regulation of institutions offering Islamic financial products and to develop, for the Islamic financial services industry, the criteria for identifying, measuring, managing and disclosing risks, taking into account international standards for valuation, income and expense calculation and disclosure

3. To liaise and cooperate with relevant organisations currently setting standards for the stability and the soundness of the international monetary and financial systems and those of the member countries

4. To enhance and coordinate initiatives to develop instruments and procedures for efficient operations and risk management

5. To encourage co-operation amongst member countries in developing the Islamic financial services industry

6. To facilitate training and personnel development and skills in areas relevant to the effective regulation of the Islamic financial services industry and related markets

7. To undertake research into, and publish studies and surveys on, the Islamic financial services industry

8. To establish a database of Islamic banks, financial institutions and industry experts

9. Any other objectives which the General Assembly of the IFSB may agree on from time to time.

What is the Liquidity Management Centre (LMC)?

Answer

The Liquidity Management Centre B.S.C. (LMC) was established on 29 July 2002 in the Kingdom of Bahrain as a Bahraini joint stock company with an Islamic Investment Banking licence.

Its principal vision is to enable Islamic financial institutions to manage their liquidity mismatches through short- and medium-term liquid investments structured in accordance with *Sharia'a* principles.

What Is the Role of the LMC?

Answer

The LMC was established for the purpose of facilitating the investment of the surplus funds of Islamic banks and financial institutions into quality short- and medium-term financial instruments, structured in accordance with *Sharia'a* principles.

The LMC is committed to playing a key role in the creation of an active and geographically expansive Islamic inter-bank market which will assist Islamic financial institutions in managing their short-term liquidity. The establishment and depth of such an inter-bank market is designed to further accelerate the development process of the Islamic banking sector. In addition, it is intended that the LMC will attract assets from governments, financial institutions and corporates in both private and public sectors in many countries. The sourced assets will be securitised into readily transferable securities or structured into other innovative investment instruments.

The LMC also offers other Islamic advisory services, including, but not limited to, the areas of structured/project/corporate finance.

What Is the International Islamic Financial Market (IIFM)?

Answer

The IIFM was founded with the collective efforts of the central banks and monetary agencies of Bahrain, Brunei, Indonesia, Malaysia, Sudan and the IDB based in Saudi Arabia, as an infrastructure institution with the mandate to promote and enhance the establishment, development, self-regulation and promotion of the Islamic capital and money markets.

The IIFM's primary focus lies in the advancement and standardisation of Islamic financial instrument structures, contracts, product development and infrastructure, and the issuance of guidelines and recommendations for the enhancement of Islamic capital and money markets globally. In addition, development of the global primary and secondary Islamic capital and short-term financial markets and the creation of a market for Islamic financial instruments are key areas for the IIFM.

What Is the Vision of the IIFM?

Answer

To create 'Active and well regulated trading and capital flows across the full spectrum of *Sharia'a* compliant and financial instruments internationally'.

What Is the Mission of the IIFM?

Answer

'To achieve the Vision by catalyzing both a national and international trading infrastructure, product innovation and information flow within strong, transparent and well-regulated standards and guidelines. Promoting acceptance and integration with mainstream markets'.

What Is the Mandate of the IIFM?

Answer

The IIFM plays an active role in the global development of Islamic capital and short-term financial markets by facilitating the introduction of professional practices, creating common platforms for market participants through various working groups and committees.

What Are the Objectives of the IIFM?

Answer

The principal objective of the IIFM is to encourage self-regulation for the development and promotion of the Islamic capital and money market segment. The IIFM, in partnership with its member institutions, creates initiatives that include issuance and trading guidelines, best practice procedures, standardisation of financial contracts leading to product innovation and market recommendations and infrastructure development. In particular, the IIFM promotes the emergence and integration of Islamic financial markets into mainstream global financial markets.

The IIFM acts as a market body in the development and maintenance of uniformity, assisting with standards benchmarking for the transparency and robustness of Islamic financial markets.

The IIFM plays an active role in the establishment, development and enhancement of trading, settlement and related systems infrastructure and involves itself with several challenging issues for Islamic financial markets. These include Islamic hedging, secondary market documentation and the creation of innovative products, for example, an Islamic repo market, treasury *Murabaha* contract mechanisms and similar elements vital to a well-developed and functional Islamic financial system.

What Is the Broader Contribution of the IIFM?

Answer

The IIFM's contribution to the Islamic financial services industry includes the following:

Market body

The IIFM forms a link between Islamic financial market participants and regulatory bodies on the Islamic capital and money market segment of the industry. Its working group's structure brings market participants onto a common platform with support from regulatory institutions.

Wider *Sharia'a* acceptance

Wider *Sharia'a* acceptance is provided through access to other *Sharia'a* Boards.

Self-regulation

Members benefit from recommendations, guidelines and best practices on primary and secondary market issues.

Uniformity and standardisation

The production of unified documentation frameworks and product development creates cost reduction for all IFIs together with improved transactional security.

Knowledge sharing

The IIFM promotes the active participation of both Islamic and Islamically interested institutions and industry professionals. This is achieved through the exchange of knowledge and expertise on a global basis through IIFM's specialised forums and workshops on Islamic capital and money markets.

Systems development

The IIFM advises on the integrity and compliance of a variety of Islamic financial infrastructures.

What Is the International Islamic Rating Agency (IIRA)?

Answer

The Islamic International Rating Agency (IIRA) is the sole rating agency established to provide capital markets and the banking sector in predominantly Islamic countries with a rating spectrum that encompasses the full array of capital instruments and speciality Islamic financial products and to enhance the level of analytical expertise in those markets.

The IIRA's augmented rating system recognises and incorporates the unique features of Islamic finance in a way that broadens the quality perspective that is a rating agency's ultimate goal. This will facilitate development of the company's markets. The business model employed, focused on the needs of institutional investors, predicates value creation for ratings on the premise that investors will ultimately demand the company's ratings and research. The IIRA is also soliciting recognition of its ratings by regulators. This business model defines the prerequisites for establishment of the agency: absolute independence of rating judgment, objective and impartial rating committees, highly trained professional analytical staff and business objectives determined by the market.

The IIRA B.S.C. started operations in July 2005 to facilitate development of the regional and national financial markets by delineating relative investment or credit risk, providing an assessment of the risk profile of entities and instruments. The IIRA is sponsored by multilateral development institutions, leading banks, other financial institutions and rating agencies. Its shareholders operate from 11 countries which constitute the agency's primary marketing focus.

The IIRA is structured in a way to preserve its independence. It has a Board of Directors and a completely independent Rating Committee. Its *Sharia'a* Board is made up of experts in the field.

What Is the Vision of the IIRA?

Answer

The vision is to become the ultimate reference point for credit ratings in accordance with *Sharia'a* principles.

What Is the Mission of the IIRA?

Answer

The mission of the IIRA is to foster development of the financial markets in which it operates through the provision of:

- ratings for sovereign bond issues;
- traditional bond/*Sukuk* ratings and a rating framework;
- *Sharia'a* quality ratings to reflect institutional compliance;
- investment quality and/or issuer ratings;
- specialist focused corporate governance ratings;
- a periodic summary bulletin of market activity and ratings;
- economic commentary from a credit and investment quality perspective;
- detailed rating reports designed to enhance the investment decision process;
- sector reports clarifying company status within industry groupings;
- a record of actual and prospective money and capital market activity;
- analysis of financial institution counterparty risk for treasurers;
- seminars on the analytical principles employed by rating agencies.

What Are the Objectives of the IIRA?

1. To develop methodologies and benchmarks for Issues/Issuer ratings
2. To provide an independent assessment and opinion on the likelihood of timely repayment of financial obligations by sovereigns, corporates, banks and financial institutions and of securities issued by governments, corporates, banks and financial institutions
3. To provide an independent opinion on the level of compliance with the principles of *Sharia'a*
4. To assess the governance system of corporates, banks and other financial institutions
5. To disseminate and publish information and data relating to business enterprises for the development of sound and efficient capital markets
6. To offer research, analysis and evaluation of sectors, industries and entities
7. To encourage the introduction of standards for greater disclosure and transparency.

Chapter 3

Why is Interest (*Riba*) Forbidden to Muslims?

> The *central tenet* of Islamic banking, the prohibition of interest, stems from the *Qur'anic* quotation below.
>
> *Sura* 275. Those who eat riba will not stand (on the Day of Resurrection) except like the standing of a person beaten by Shaitân (Satan) leading him to insanity. That is because they say: "Trading is only like Riba," whereas Allah has permitted trading and forbidden riba. So whosoever receives an admonition from his Lord and stops eating riba shall not be punished for the past; his case is for Allah (to judge); but whoever returns [to riba], such are the dwellers of the Fire – they will abide therein.
>
> The *Qur'an* – *Al-Baqarah S.275–281*

In fact, the prohibition of interest (*riba*) is mentioned in four different revelations in the *Qur'an*. The first revelation emphasizes that interest deprives wealth of God's blessings. The second revelation condemns it, placing interest in juxtaposition with the wrongful appropriation of property belonging to others. The third revelation enjoins Muslims to stay clear of interest for the sake of their own welfare. The fourth revelation establishes a clear distinction between interest and trade, urging Muslims to take only the principal sum and to forgo even this sum if the borrower is unable to repay. It is further declared, in the *Qur'an*, that those who disregard the prohibition of interest are at war with God and His Prophet.

Riba in the Qur'an and the Sunnah/Hadith

The Islamic prohibition of interest (*riba*) is so central to the Islamic banking system that it is essential to understand why this is so and what the implications are.

Riba comes in two varieties:

1. ***Riba Al-Nasiah*** – interest on borrowed money
2. ***Riba Al-Fadl*** – exchanging a superior thing of the same
   kind of goods by giving more of the same kind of goods of
   inferior quality, e.g. dates of superior quality for dates of
   inferior quality.

The literal meaning of interest or *riba*, as it is used in Arabic, means an excess or increase. In the Islamic terminology
interest means effortless profit. *Riba* has been described as a
loan with the condition that the borrower will return to the
lender more than the amount borrowed.

One of the main concerns of Muslims, when it comes to
financial transactions, is to avoid *Riba* in any of its forms.
This is despite the fact that the basic foundation of modern
business and finance involves interest-based transactions.

The Prophet Mohammed foretold of a time when the
spread of *riba* would be so overwhelming that it would be
extremely difficult for Muslims to avoid it. This situation
calls for Muslims to be extra cautious before deciding on
what financial methods to use in any personal or business
transaction.

To understand why the ban on interest is so central to
Islamic finance it is essential to examine the textual evidence.

What Is the Textual Evidence for the Ban on Interest?

The Qur'an – Al-Baqarah S.275–281

> *Sura* 275. Those who eat Riba will not stand (on the Day
> of Resurrection) except like the standing of a person

beaten by Shaitân (Satan) leading him to insanity. That is because they say: "Trading is only like Riba," whereas Allah has permitted trading and forbidden Riba. So whosoever receives an admonition from his Lord and stops eating Riba shall not be punished for the past; his case is for Allah (to judge); but whoever returns [to Riba], such are the dwellers of the Fire - they will abide therein.

Sura 276. Allah will destroy Riba and will give increase for Sadaqât (deeds of charity, alms, etc.) And Allah likes not the disbelievers, sinners.

Sura 277. Truly those who believe, and do deeds of righteousness, and perform As-Salat (Prayer), and give Zakat (an obligatory religious tax), they will have their reward with their Lord. On them shall be no fear, nor shall they grieve.

Sura 278. O you who believe! Be afraid of Allah and give up what remains (due to you) from Riba (from now onward), if you are (really) believers.

Sura 279. And if you do not do it, then take a notice of war from Allah and His Messenger but if you repent, you shall have your capital sums. Deal not unjustly (by asking more than your capital sums), and you shall not be dealt with unjustly (by receiving less than your capital sums).

Sura 280. And if the debtor is in a hard time (i.e. has no money), then grant him time till it is easy for him to repay, but if you remit it by way of charity, that is better for you if you did but know.

Sura 281. And be afraid of the Day when you shall be brought back to Allah. Then every person shall be paid what he earned, and they shall not be dealt with unjustly.

The Qur'an – Al-Imran S.3: 130

O you who believe! Eat not Riba doubled and multiplied, but fear Allah that you may be successful.

Hadith – Sahih Bukhari, Volume 3, No. 299; Narrated by 'Aun bin Abu Juhaifah, r.a.

My father bought a slave who practised the profession of cupping (defined below). My father broke the servant's instruments of cupping. I asked my father why he had done so. He replied, "The Prophet forbade the acceptance of the price of a dog or blood, and also forbade the profession of tattooing, or getting tattooed and receiving or giving Riba, and cursed the picture makers."

(Cupping means letting out bad blood that lies just beneath the skin. It is a type of medical treatment.)

Hadith – Sahih Bukhari, 2.468, Narrated by Samura bin Jundab, r.a.

He speaks of in a dream related to the Prophet that there is a river of blood and a man was in it, and another man was standing at its bank with stones in front of him, facing the man standing in the river. Whenever the man in the river wanted to come out, the other one threw a stone at his mouth and caused him to retreat back into his original position. The Prophet was told that these people, in this river of blood, were people who dealt in Riba.

Hadith – Mishkat-ul-Masabih

The following three *ahadith* have been taken from *Mishkat-ul-Masabih* under the section of interest. The English translation has been taken from its English version written by Al Hajj Moulana Fazl Karim (218–227 vol. 11).

- Hazrat Jabir has reported that the Messenger of Allah cursed the devourer of usury, its payer, its scribe and its two witnesses. He also said that they were equal (in sin).
- Hazrat Abu Hurairah reported that the Prophet said: A time will certainly come over the people when none will remain who will not devour usury. If he does not devour it, its vapour will overtake him. [Ahmed, Abu Dawood, Nisai, Ibn Majah]
- Hazrat Abu Hurairah reported that the Messenger of Allah said: I came across some people in the night in which I was taken to the heavens. Their stomachs were like houses wherein there were serpents, which could be seen from the front of the stomachs. I asked: O Gabriel! Who are these people? He replied these are those who devoured usury. [Ahmed, Ibn Majah]

Hadith – Hazrat Al-Khudri reported that the Prophet said: Gold in exchange for gold, silver in exchange for silver, wheat in exchange for wheat, barley in exchange for barley, dates in exchange for dates, salt in exchange for salt is in the same category and (should be exchanged) hand to hand, so whoever adds or demands increase he has practised usury. The giver and taker are the same.

Conclusion on the Textual Evidence

It is evident from the textual evidence that interest is *haram* (prohibited) for Muslims. Allah has declared war on the user. Islam encourages men to earn their own provision and provide for their families on the condition that the earnings are in accord with the *Sharia'a*.

While the basic source of the ban on the use of interest is the divine authority of the *Qur'an*, somewhat surprisingly, no

Qur'anic-based rationale was provided for why this was the case. It is this issue to which I now turn.

What is the Islamic rationale for banning interest (riba)?

One of the main features that distinguishes Islamic financial institutions from their conventional banking counterparts is that Islamic institutions adhere closely to the Islamic creed (*aqidah*). Since those institutions are first and foremost Muslim institutions, they share the fundamental Islamic drive to avoid what Allah has forbidden. In this regard, the *Qur'an* contains clear and eternal prohibitions of all kinds of *riba*, whether sales or loan related.

In this context we read, as mentioned earlier: 'But indeed Allah has permitted trade and forbidden riba' (2:275). The *Qur'an* also states that Allah has ordered Muslims to abandon and liquidate all remaining riba (regardless of how large or small): 'O you who believe, fear Allah and give up what remains of riba, if you are indeed believers' (2:278), and declare war on those who devour it: 'If you do not, take notice of a war from Allah and his Messenger; but if you turn back then you shall have your principal (without interest) without inflicting or receiving injustice' (2:279).

To deserve such a declaration of war is the severest punishment in all of Islam, providing further proof that *riba* is one of the most severely forbidden of transgressions.

There is no ambiguity about the impermissibility of riba within the Islamic financial system

The primary rationale for abolishing interest and for introducing Islamic banking principles is a religious one, and it is therefore difficult to evaluate the reasoning in purely secular terms. Nevertheless, Islamic scholars have sought to provide a theoretical basis for the prohibition in terms of morality and economics.

Five reasons have been put forward by Islamic scholars for the prohibition of *riba*:

1. It is unjust.
2. It corrupts society.
3. It implies improper appropriation of other people's property.
4. Ultimately it results in negative economic growth.
5. It demeans and diminishes human personality.

1. Interest is unjust

Among the most important reasons that have been emphasised by most Islamic scholars is that interest is prohibited because it is unjust (*zulm*). A contract based on interest involves injustice to one of the parties, sometimes to the lender and sometimes to the borrower.

Sura 2:279 clearly states that taking an amount in excess of the principal would be unjust. It also recognises the right of the lender/creditor to the principal without any decrease as that too would be unjust. The *Qur'an* does not rationalise, however, as to why it is unfair to take an excess in the case of a loan. Presumably, it relies on the notions of equality and reciprocity inherent in the Islamic concept of justice.

The unacceptability of injustice and unfairness was never in dispute between the *Qur'an* and its audience. What is not immediately understandable, to non-Muslims, is the Qur'anic stand that taking anything in excess of the principal amounts to injustice. This needs to be explained.

The *riba* contract is deemed to be unjust to the borrower because if somebody takes a loan and uses it in his business he may earn a profit or he may end up with a loss. In the case of a loss the entrepreneur will have received no return for his time and work. In addition to this loss, he has to pay interest and capital to the lender. The lender, or the financier, in spite of the fact that the business has ended up making a loss gets his capital returned as well as his interest. It is in this context that *riba* is deemed unjust.

The *Qur'an* makes clear that individuals having difficulty paying their debts should have their obligations made easier for them and not more difficult. Such individuals may actually deserve charity and it is a morally offensive practice to start demanding that they be punished for their failure to pay on time.

Riba, derived from this rationalisation in the Prophet's last sermon, is the crime of a party which is owed money demanding an 'increase in a debt' owed to them as a compensation for late payment. The reason for this delay may be that the lender has suffered some financial problem but, Islamic scholars argue, a judge must consider the debtor's situation first. If payment is late without good reason and there was no difficulty in making the payment, then demands of payment of additional damages may be legitimate, but this is a matter of judgment for a judge and it is not for one party to be able to impose their desired punishment on the other. Automatic penalties built into contracts are also unjust for the same reason. For damages to be legitimate, it is argued, they must be based on the claim of wilful breach of contract and decided by a judge. Failure to pay may be due to difficulty of circumstances and therefore, it is argued, not something simply willed by the debtor.

There are thus two related aspects to the practice of *riba* as referred to by the Prophet and the *Qur'an* that make it unjust:

1. Punishing someone for default is unjust.
2. It should be a judge who decides what the compensation for a default should be, not the party to whom the debt is owed.

This latter aspect is crucial, it is argued, because once a jurisdiction allows for contracts to impose punishments for default, then the law itself becomes nothing but the slave of such contracts and any crime may be legitimised as a form of punishment of the 'debt-slave'. A relationship in which one party imposes punishment on another is that of a master and a slave. The relationship in which one party buys something from another should be a relationship of equals.

2. Interest corrupts society

The argument here is that there is an association between charging interest with *fasad*, loosely translated as the corruption of society. This argument is revealed from *Sura* 30, *Ar-Rum*, along with some of the preceding and following verses. These read as follows:

> That which you give in usury in order that it may increase in other people's property has no increase with Allah; but that which you give in charity, seeking Allah's countenance, has increased manifold. Allah is He Who created you and then sustained you, then causes you to die, then gives life to you again. Is there any of your (so called) partners (of Allah) that does aught of that? Praised and exalted be He above what they associate with him. Corruption does appear on land and sea because of (the evil) which men's hands have done, that He may make them taste a part of that which they have done, in order that they may return.
>
> (S.30: 37–41)

Within the framework of the general message that *fasad* (illegal acts under Islam) in society results from men's own (wrong) behaviour, we can clearly read the sub-message that charging interest is one of those facets of wrong behaviour that corrupts society. In fact this may have been the first time, chronologically speaking, that *riba* is mentioned in the *Qur'an*. It was in the fitness of things to highlight its negative social role long before the practice of charging interest was banned.

3. Interest implies unlawful appropriation of other people's property

The reasoning here is indicated in the verse from *Sura* 4, *Au-Nisa*. In that verse, the Jews are admonished for 'taking usury when they were forbidden it, and of their devouring people's wealth by false pretences' (S.4:161). Significantly, the *Qur'an* relates the tendency to appropriate other people's wealth without any justification, to some more serious crimes. In *Sura* 9:34 *riba* is associated with hoarding and *Sura* 4:29 seems to put it at par with murder.

Considering the serious dimensions of *fasad* to which *riba* has been related, the message seems to be clear: charging interest belongs to a mindset that leads to the disruption of civil society.

The argument here is that interest on money is regarded as representing an unjustified creation of instantaneous property rights. It is unjustified, because interest is a property right claimed outside the legitimate framework of recognised property rights. It is instantaneous because as soon as the contract for lending upon interest is concluded, a right to the borrower's property is created for the lender. This is what the provision of collateral is all about.

4. Ultimate effect of interest-based systems is negative growth

The fourth reason is implied in the declaration that *riba* is subject to destruction (*mahq*) S. 2:276 which means decrease after decrease, a continuous process of diminishing. That sounds a little odd as it runs counter to the commonly observed fact of people growing rich by applying the power of compound interest. Once we leave out the improbable interpretation of individual wealth amassed through *riba* business being subject to continuous decrease, we have to turn to an alternative interpretation, namely, its effect on social wealth.

Riba, even when it is increasing in numerical terms, it is argued, fails to spur growth in social wealth. That role is played by charitable giving mentioned in the next half of *Sura* 2:276. Charitable giving transfers purchasing power to the poor and the needy who are dependent upon it. The destination of interest earnings is not that certain.

Interest, it is argued, also has many adverse consequences for the economy. It results in an inefficient allocation of society's resources, and can contribute to the instability of the system. In an interest-based system, the major criterion for the distribution of credit is the credit-worthiness of the borrower. In an Islamic finance-sharing system the productivity of the project is more important, thereby encouraging finance to go to more productive projects. In this way, instead of resources going to low-return projects for borrowers with better credit-worthiness, bank lending is more likely to flow to high-return projects even if the credit-worthiness of the borrower is somewhat lower. Therefore, the Islamic-sharing system is potentially more efficient in allocating resources.

It is also deemed to be more efficient because the return to the bank is now linked to the success of the project. In the interest-based system banks do not have to care as much about project evaluation, it is argued, since they obtain a return on their loans irrespective of the success of the project.

Also, in conventional banking if security is provided then a return is guaranteed (or at least part guaranteed) even if the project is a disaster. While conventional banks, of course, make losses, the argument is that interest-based systems force borrowers to continue to repay loans even when their circumstances are ill-suited to making such repayments, ultimately exacerbating the problem and resulting in default. Interest-based banking systems, therefore, may accentuate downturns in the business cycle.

5. Interest demeans and diminishes human personality

The fifth reason behind the prohibition of *riba* is inferred from *Sura* 2:275 quoted above. This verse draws a picture of 'those who devour usury' as well as states the reason why they get into that pitiable mould, as Muslims would see it. That reason is their being trapped into the false economics that equates trade – the act of selling and buying – with the practice of charging interest.

In many cases, the charging of interest is also demeaning. For example, if the loan is for procuring things necessary for survival, charging interest violates the nature of social life which requires cooperation, care and help for the needy from those who can spare the money.

One may legitimately ask how earning interest can affect your personality? A plausible answer lies in the generally rising level of anxiety in modern interest-based societies. The fact of the matter is that in the complex modern economy the relationship between the one who pays interest and the one who receives interest is not as direct and visible as in the primitive agricultural societies or merchant communities of old. It is mediated by numerous agencies and institutions, which makes it impersonal, potentially raising anxiety levels.

Chapter 4
Derivatives and Islamic Finance

*W*hether derivatives are permissible in Islamic finance has become the subject of heated debate between scholars, academics and banking practitioners. To appreciate the issues so hotly debated, it is essential to go back to the primary sources of *Sharia'a* Law.

The controversies revolve around gambling, the Arabic term for which is *maisir*.

Definition of Maisir

Maisir means a game involving hazardous events – particularly a game of chance played by means of divining arrows, defined below. This was a popular game at the time of the Prophet Mohammed. *Maisir* comes in various categories. Some of these types of *maisir* are seeking omens or fortune telling by divining arrows, playing backgammon, chess, lotteries, and so on.

The word *maisir* (game of chance) is derived from the root:

1. *Yasara*: to become gentle, to draw lots by arrows;
2. *Yasara*: affluence because *maisir* brings about profit;
3. *Yusr*: convenience, ease. M*aisir* is so termed because it is a means of making money without toil and exertion;
4. *Yasr*: dividing a thing into a number of shares and distributing them among themselves. Gambling is called *maisir* because those who partake in the games of chance divide the meat of sacrificial animals amongst themselves.

All the above connotations are vividly found in the word *maisir*. Imam Malik, founder of the Maliki School of jurisprudence, said that gambling was of two categories: a game of chance that is partaken in with a view to sport (fun) and the game of chance which involves gambling. Gambling, in this sense, means all dealings in which people are required to make a bet. Every dealing which involves some aspect of gambling is *maisir*. So where does gambling fit within the *Qur'an*?

The Qur'an on the Prohibition of Gambling

They ask thee (O' Prophet) about *Khamr* (intoxicants) and games of chance (gambling). Say: In both of them there is great harm although there is some advantage as well in them for men, but their harm is much greater than their advantages.

Sura 2:219

O' ye who believe, verily wine and games of chance, (ungodly) shrines, and divining devices are abomination of Satan's work. Avoid them, that ye may prosper. Only would Satan sow hatred and strife among you, by wine, and games of chance, and turn you aside from the remembrance of Allah, and from Prayer: Will you not, therefore, abstain from them?

Sura 5:90, 91

Through these verses of the *Qur'an*, it is also made clear that games of chance (*maisir*) entail sin whilst promising petty benefits. In fact *maisir*, based on the above citations, is deemed by Muslims to be an abominable act of Satan. It is therefore imperative, for Muslims, to avoid gambling in order to achieve success and happiness. Satan, it is believed, through games of chance, sows in the hearts of Muslims the seeds of enmity and hatred against one another and turns believers aside from the remembrance of Allah and His worship. The prohibition of gambling has, therefore, been declared obligatory.

Ahadith on the prohibition of gambling

The Prophet said: 'Whosoever says to his Companion: Come let us place a game of haphazard, should give alms (as atonement).'

Bukhari and Muslim

It connotes that a mere invitation to gambling is such a serious sin as to warrant atonement thereof by charity. Then just imagine the position of a man who indulges in gambling. The Holy Prophet further said: 'Whosoever plays backgammon is as if he dyes his hands with the flesh of swine and its blood.'

Muslim

Ibn Abi Al-Dunya has reported that Yahya b Kathir commented on people playing backgammon, 'Their hearts are pre-occupied in sport, their hands are ill and (their) tongues make absurd utterances. Every game which involves gambling or mischief is a game of chance (*maisir*).'

Some exceptions to the prohibition

There is no difference of opinion among the jurists that every sort of gambling is harmful, except betting for horse racing and archery. These have been declared lawful in order to encourage horsemanship, archery and preparation for *Jihad*. This is because Allah says:

Make ready for them all you can of (armed) force and of horses tethered, that thereby ye may dismay the enemy of Allah and your enemy.

Surah 8:60

Stone Altars, Gambling and Jahiliya

Stone altars were erected round the Holy *Ka'ba* in the pre-Islamic period (known as *Jahiliya*, the period of ignorance).

People used to slaughter their sacrificial animals beside these altars. Such altars were around 360 in number. Around the stone altars various forms of gambling took place.

With the advent of Islam, these altars were removed. This dismantlement of altars took place on the eve of the victory of Mecca when the Holy Prophet climbed on them with a staff in hand and demolished them one after the other and recited this *Qur'anic* verse:

> And say: Truth hath come and falsehood hath vanished away. Lo, falsehood is ever bound to vanish.
>
> *Sura* 17:81

A Brief History of the Prohibition of Gambling in Islam

The history of the unlawfulness of the games of chance, namely, gambling in Islam, is as old as the history of the unlawfulness of wine because the prohibition of both was declared simultaneously in *Sura al-Baqara* (2:219) and *Sura al-Ma'ida* (5:90, 91), as already mentioned.

The first stage was the revelation of *Sura* 2:219 in the month of *Rabi-ul-Awwal*, 4 AH (August AD 625). Allah, in this verse, mentioned the game of chance (*maisir*) as characteristic of great sin which has paltry benefits for mankind. This verse is, therefore, a clear proof of the gradual prohibition of games of chance.

The second and the last stage is the revelation of *Sura* 5:90, 91 in the month of *Dhi-al-Qa'da*, 6 AH (March, AD 627). In these verses, Allah totally declared gambling (*maisir*) unlawful, leaving no room for relaxation.

Nature of Gambling and the Arabs

In pre-Islamic times when famine broke out the Arabs brought sacrificial animals – camels and sheep – and slaughtered them. Then they divided them into 28 shares and placed 10 arrows near them, namely, *fadh, tawam, raqib, hils, nafis, musbil, mu'alli, manih, sanih* and *waghd*.

One out of these 28 shares was earmarked for *fadh*, two for *tawam*, three for *raqib*, four for *hils*, five for *nafis*, six for *musbil* and seven for *mu'alli*. *Mu'alli* would receive a major share and from this a proverb came into vogue. Everyone who would have a lion's share of anything was called '*Sahibu al-qidhil mu'alli*. The last three arrows *manih, sanih* and *waghd* had no share at all. This process was completed among 10 persons, in effect, drawing lots.

The Arabs then distributed these shares among the needy and they themselves did not eat anything out of them. They felt proud of that act and condemned those who did not participate in this ritual. The latter were nicknamed as '*baram*', that is, a mean and niggardly man devoid of manly traits. Later on, they replaced the spirit of the ritual and made the arrows a means of business without any consideration of munificence and help to the needy. Later men began to gamble with all their property and as a result risked becoming destitute and penniless.

Divining Arrows for Seeking Fortune

During pre-Islamic times, the Arabs used to make 10 arrows, as mentioned above, which were strips of wood without headpoints. They named them *aqlam* (pen-sticks), *qidah* (featherless arrows) and *azlam* (divinatory arrows), which were put in a *ribabah* or leather bag. Divining arrows (*azlam*) are arrows cut off from thin slices of wood in the shape of arrows having no heads.

The gambling format involved paying the stake money and putting one's hand in the leather bag to bring out an arrow which would be in the name of a polytheist, and so on. If an arrow having some share was brought out by someone, he took the share specified for it and if an arrow having no share was brought out by someone he would not get anything and would lose his entire stake money.

There were two other kinds of seeking fortune and both of them involved securing some information about unseen events. The first category was one whereby the keeper of the Holy *Ka'ba* had three arrows. On one of them was written 'Do', on the second arrow was written 'Do not do', while on the third one nothing was written. According to another report of the same event on one arrow was written 'My Lord hath commanded me', on the second arrow was written 'My Lord hath forbidden me', while the third one carried no remarks whatsoever. Whenever anyone intended to go on some journey, make war, wanted to marry, make a business transaction or wanted to go away for some other reason, the custodian of the *Ka'ba* would cast the divining arrows. If the arrow having the words 'My Lord hath commanded me' came out, the recipient would get on with whatever he wanted to do. On the other hand, if the arrow with the words 'My Lord hath forbidden me' was selected he would desist from going on his proposed endeavour. If the arrow which bore no words was drawn, the above process was repeated.

The second category involved foreseeing future events and gambling using arrows. One of them was near the idol called *Hubal* placed inside the Holy *Ka'ba*. All the vicissitudes with which humanity comes across were inscribed on this arrow and the Arabs cast lots by means of it, in the manner already discussed. As can be seen, *Qur'anic* citations on the perils of gambling are numerous.

Allah has forbidden all the gambling means of seeking fortune in the verse:

> Forbidden it is that ye seek fortune by divining arrows. This is an abomination.
>
> *Sura* 5:3

Similarly other verses have also been revealed in the *Qur'an*.

The rationale underlying the prohibition of seeking fortune by arrows is that it is seen as an absurd and superstitious action which is most certainly deemed un-Islamic. The act of seeking one's fortune by arrow heads leads, it is argued, to a claim of the knowledge of the unseen. This power, Muslims believe, exclusively vests in Allah. These omens of fortune were sought from the flight of birds, divination, augury, geomancy, sorcery, magic and astronomy. All these techniques, to succeed, involve prior knowledge of the future, the unseen.

All of these acts are unlawful in the sight of the *Sharia'a*. As the *Qur'an* says:

> Say (O' Prophet): None in the heavens and the earth knoweth the unseen save Allah.
>
> *Sura* 27:65

Again, the *Qur'an* says:

> And it is not (the purpose of) Allah to let you know the unseen.
>
> *Sura* 3:179

In conclusion, derivatives, widely seen by Muslims as forms of gambling, are unequivocally condemned. Investment bankers are desperately attempting to structure Islamically acceptable forms of derivatives. They are fighting an uphill struggle!

Chapter 5

How do you Establish an Islamic Bank?

The Islamic Bank of Britain (IBB)

*G*iven the rapid growth of Islamic banking many conventional banks are considering entering the industry. But just how do you do it and what lessons can we learn from newcomers to the industry?

The creation of the Islamic Bank of Britain (IBB) was a pioneering event in the development of the western banking system. The IBB was the first fully-fledged Islamic bank to be opened in the European Union and provides an illuminating case study for other potential entrants to the industry.

The crux of the Islamic economic system is the sharing of profits and losses. All the liabilities and assets in the balance sheet of an Islamic bank are risk capital. In the conventional banking system, the value of deposits is guaranteed by the bank, plus there is a guarantee of the payment of interest.

This chapter examines the issues involved in opening an Islamic bank subject to a western regulatory framework. It examines the procedures as seen through the viewpoint of the UK regulatory body, the Financial Services Authority (FSA). The issues were varied, covering non-payment of interest, the differing banking products made available, the role of deposit protection and many other related issues.

Background

Authorisation of the Islamic Bank of Britain

In August 2004, the FSA authorised the IBB, the first wholly Islamic retail bank in the United Kingdom, a country where most of the population is non-Muslim. Inevitably, the process raised many new issues and it took some 18–24 months to complete. The FSA was then able to carry over the lessons to later Islamic banking licence applications.

The main issue that arose concerned the definition of a 'deposit'. In the United Kingdom, a *deposit* is defined by the FSA as a 'sum of money paid on terms under which it will be repaid either on demand or in circumstances agreed by parties'. This point is important because deposit-takers are regulated and the customer is assured of full repayment as long as the bank remains solvent. A savings account originally proposed by IBB as a deposit was a profit and loss sharing account, or *Mudaraba*, where *Sharia'a* law requires the customer to accept the risk of loss of original capital. This was not consistent with the FSA's interpretation of the legal definition of a deposit which requires capital certainty.

After extensive discussions with the FSA, the solution IBB adopted was to accept that, legally, its depositors are entitled to full repayment, thus ensuring compliance with FSA requirements. However, customers have the right to turn down deposit protection, after the event, on religious grounds, and choose instead to be repaid under the *Sharia'a*-compliant risk-sharing and loss-bearing formula.

The FSA's Approach to Authorisation

The Financial Services and Markets Act 2000

Anyone seeking to conduct a regulated activity in the United Kingdom is required to apply to the FSA for permission under Part IV of the Financial Services and Markets Act 2000 (FSMA). The FSMA deals with the regulation of financial services in the United Kingdom and is the legislation under which corporate bodies, partnerships, individuals and unincorporated associations are permitted, by the FSA, to carry on those financial activities which are subject to regulation.

Under Section 19 of the FSMA, any person who carries on a regulated activity in the United Kingdom must be authorised by the FSA or be exempt. A breach of Section 19 may be a criminal offence.

Regulated activities

The activities that are subject to regulation are specified in the Financial Services and Markets Act 2000 (Regulated Activities) Order 2001 (RAO). Examples include accepting deposits, effecting or carrying out contracts of insurance and advising on investments.

Before the FSA was established as the single financial regulator in the United Kingdom, several separate regulators oversaw different financial markets. The Bank of England, for example, was responsible for supervising banks under the Banking Act 1987 and the Securities and Investment Board was responsible, under the 1986 Financial Services Act, for investment regulation which was carried out by several self-regulatory organisations. However, under the FSMA and subject to any specific restrictions, firms now seek a scope of permission from the FSA to be authorised for the full range of regulated activities they wish to undertake.

Most of the Islamic applications the FSA has received so far have been to establish Islamic banks. Banking itself is not a defined regulated activity; rather, the generally understood meaning is of an entity which undertakes the regulated activity of 'accepting deposits' (and is not a credit union, building society, friendly society or insurance company). As defined by the RAO, this covers money received by way of deposit lent to others or any other activity of the person accepting the deposit which is financed, wholly or to any material extent, out of the capital of, or interest on, money received by way of deposit. This activity warrants classification as a credit institution under the EU Banking

Consolidation Directive and firms undertaking it are subject to the appropriate capital requirements. A firm claiming to be a bank will therefore be expected to seek this activity within the scope of its permission.

Non-discriminatory regime

All financial institutions authorised by the FSA and operating in the United Kingdom, or seeking to do so, are subject to the same standards. This is true regardless of their country of origin, the sectors in which they wish to specialise or their religious principles. This approach is fully consistent with the FSMA's six Principles of Good Regulation, in particular, facilitating innovation and avoiding unnecessary barriers to entry or expansion within the financial markets.

There is, therefore, as stressed by the FSA, a 'level playing field' in dealing with applications from conventional and Islamic firms. The FSA is happy to see Islamic finance develop in the United Kingdom, but they stress that it would not be appropriate, nor would it be legally possible, to vary its standards for one particular type of institution. The FSA's approach can be summed up as 'no obstacles, but no special favours'.

Authorisation requirements

All firms seeking FSA authorisation are required to provide a credible business plan and meet, and continue to meet, five basic requirements known as the *Threshold Conditions*.

In summary, the five conditions are as follows:

1. The firm must have the correct legal status for the activities it wishes to undertake. This recognises, for example, that European directives place certain limits on

the legal form that a firm accepting deposits or effecting and carrying out contracts of insurance may take.

2. For a firm incorporated in the United Kingdom, its head office and *mind and management* must also be in the United Kingdom.

3. If the person or firm has *close links* with another person or firm, then these are not thought likely to prevent the effective supervision of the firm.

4. The firm has adequate resources, both financial and non-financial, for the activities which it seeks to carry on.

5. The firm is 'fit and proper'. This takes into account its connection with other persons, including employees and shareholders, the nature of the activities it wishes to undertake and the need to conduct its affairs in a sound and prudent manner.

These conditions can readily be applied to any type of firm, although the exact requirements may need to be shaped to fit differing sectors. For example, the requirement for adequate resources, which includes capital, would be different for a bank and an insurance company. However, the capital requirements for an Islamic and a conventional bank would be applied following the same basis.

Another example would relate to the requirement that a business must have reasonable systems and controls to manage the type of business it wishes to undertake. In this case, the threshold conditions are flexible enough to be as readily applied to an Islamic firm as to a conventional provider, whatever sector the firm is operating in.

Applying the FSMA

In applying the FSMA to Islamic firms, there are several areas where more work or clarification is needed than would be usual for a conventional product.

The FSA has identified three main areas of potential difficulty which are common to the applications from Islamic financial institutions.

These are the regulatory definition of products; the role of *Sharia'a* scholars; and financial promotions.

1. Regulatory definition of products

The definition of products offered by Islamic firms is a key factor that firms and the FSA need to consider as part of the authorisation process. The structure of Islamic products is based on a set of contracts acceptable under *Sharia'a* law. So, while their economic effect is similar to or the same as conventional products, their underlying structure may, and in fact are, significantly different. This means the definition of these products under the RAO may not be the same as the conventional equivalent.

This has two important implications for applicants. Firstly, firms need to be sure they apply for the correct scope of permission for the regulated activities they wish to undertake. This, in turn, highlights the need for firms to assess whether the structure of Islamic products can be accommodated within the RAO.

Secondly, the regulatory definition is relevant in determining the framework in which products can be sold, for example, in the application or otherwise of conduct of business rules. If a product falls outside the FSA's regulatory framework, there may be restrictions on whom the product can be sold to. For these reasons, new applicants are encouraged to engage, at an early stage, with the FSA and their legal advisers about the regulatory definition of the products they intend to offer.

2. The role of Sharia'a scholars

The FSA also has to consider the role of the *Sharia'a* Supervisory Board (SSB). The industry defines the key objective of SSB scholars as ensuring *Sharia'a* compliance in all of an entity's products and transactions. In practice, *Sharia'a* scholars examine a new product or transaction and, if satisfied it is *Sharia'a*-compliant, issue an approval (*fatwa*).

The FSA is, however, a secular and not a religious regulator. It would not be appropriate, even if it were possible, for the FSA to judge between different interpretations of *Sharia'a* law. However, the FSA does need to know, from a financial and operational perspective, exactly what the role of the SSB is in each authorised firm. It needs, in particular, to know whether, and if so how, the SSB affects the running of the firm. The FSA has to be clear as to whether the *Sharia'a* scholars have an executive role or one that is simply advisory.

Why does this matter? This matters for two reasons. Firstly, in the United Kingdom, any person acting as a director of an authorised firm must be registered under the FSA Approved Persons rules. To assess the suitability of a person, the FSA has a standard known as the *Fit and Proper test for Approved Persons*. One of the factors looked at is 'competence and capability'. So, for an individual to become a director of an authorised firm, the FSA would expect him to have relevant experience. If, therefore, *Sharia'a* scholars are seen to have a directorship role, it is possible that some of them may not meet the competency and capability requirements.

Secondly, assuming that *Sharia'a* scholars are directors, their role is more likely to resemble that of an executive director than a non-executive director as it might involve active participation in the firm's business. In such cases, it would be very difficult to justify multiple memberships of SSBs of different scholars because of significant conflicts of interests. If this is strictly applied, it would put further constraints on an industry already facing a shortage of *Sharia'a* scholars with suitable skills.

The key point from the FSA's perspective is that firms can successfully show that the role and responsibilities of their SSB are advisory and their role does not interfere in the management of the firm. The firms already authorised have been able to show this. The factors that the FSA typically looks at with regard to SSBs include the governance structure, reporting lines, fee structure and the terms and conditions of the SSB's contracts.

On a related point, complex products, having gone through a long process of internal development, are sometimes rejected by the SSB for non-compliance with *Sharia'a*. To some extent, this is seen to be a result of the lack of *Sharia'a* knowledge internally in the firm. One solution put forward by some practitioners is greater involvement by *Sharia'a* scholars in the product development process. While this may prove beneficial, it could lead to a more executive role as outlined above. A good industry practice now developing is that firms are starting to recruit more staff with an understanding of *Sharia'a* law. This could help to identify a product's potential non-compliance with *Sharia'a* at a much earlier stage.

3. Financial promotions

The third issue, financial promotions, is more relevant on the retail side. Reflecting its statutory objective to protect consumers, the FSA's requirement is that all advertising should be 'clear, fair and not misleading'. This has been important in the context of Islamic finance as the products are still new and their structure differs from more conventional products. This, together with the fact that by necessity those who will wish to use them may be relatively inexperienced in financial services, reinforces the need for the promotion of Islamic financial products to include the risks as well as the benefits. The IBB case below shows how these issues have been dealt with in practice.

Authorisation of the Islamic Bank of Britain

A working group chaired by the late Eddie George (formerly the Governor of the Bank of England) considered the barriers to Islamic mortgages in the United Kingdom. The greatest barrier appeared to be the fact that Islamic mortgages attracted stamp duty on the purchase of the property by the bank and on the transfer of the property by the bank to the customer at the end of the mortgage term. The FSA, therefore, welcomed the UK government's reform in 2003, which made stamp duty payable only once.

All firms that wish to carry on a regulated financial service in the United Kingdom must obtain FSA authorisation. The process can be quite lengthy with applications taking up to six months once the FSA has received the formal application. Any application for authorisation to the FSA, whether by a conventional or an Islamic bank, requires a credible and well thought-out business plan. Applicants are expected to have conducted proper market research to assess the market appetite for their products as well as the risks such products present to consumers. The FSA was conscious that the IBB's application for authorisation was the first Islamic banking application in the United Kingdom, and, crucially, was able to be flexible within the confines of its own rules.

Issues addressed by the FSA

The FSA identified five specific issues arising in the context of Islamic banking.

1. risks in Islamic operations;
2. the FSA's definition of deposits;

3. *Sharia'a* compliance and the role of the *Sharia'a* Supervisory Board, a body unique to Islamic firms;
4. regulation of Islamic products, such as Islamic mortgages; and
5. corporate governance in Islamic firms.

1. Risks in Islamic operations
There are added risks and complications in Islamic banking caused by the need to ensure full *Sharia'a* compliance at all times. The FSA recognised such risks but did not consider them to be so substantial that they would prevent authorisation. The FSA need only to be satisfied that an Islamic bank has taken all necessary steps to mitigate such risks.

2. The FSA's definition of deposits
The main issue arising in the context of Islamic banking is the definition of deposits. In the United Kingdom, a *deposit* is defined as a 'sum of money paid on terms under which it will be repaid either on demand or in circumstances agreed by the parties'. This point is important because deposit-takers are regulated and the customer is assured that full repayment provided the bank remains solvent. The FSA's interpretation, in line with other developed legal systems, requires capital certainty. Unless the bank is actually insolvent, it must return the customer's original money to him in full, together with the return earned on it. However, if capital certainty is not assured, the bank is subject to more extensive obligations to treat customers fairly and to explain how the product operates.

The FSA had to categorise the following two types of Islamic savings accounts as either deposits or 'investments':

- a simple non-interest-bearing account, where the bank promises capital repayment; and
- a profit and loss sharing account, a *Mudaraba*, where *Sharia'a* law requires that the customer accepts the risk of loss of his original capital.

Islamic banks ideally want their profit and loss sharing accounts to be treated as deposits so that they are in a position to compete with conventional banks.

In the case of the IBB product, the solution for the bank was to offer its customer full repayment of the investment, thus ensuring full compliance with the legal definition of a deposit. However, the bank will calculate the amount of the repayment to comply with the risk-sharing formulation, and the customer need not accept repayment in full.

Islamic complications. Islamic principles of finance can produce surprises. Straightforward current accounts (checking accounts) provided by banks are sufficiently well established in the lexicon of Islamic finance for such accounts to be uncontentious. They are intrinsically *Sharia'a* compliant. The same cannot be said to be true of bank deposit accounts. From a *Sharia'a* perspective, the customer needs to be sharing risk with the bank.

From a UK bank deposit perspective, such an arrangement cannot constitute a bank deposit as it is inimical to the statutory scheme for protecting bank deposits for customers to be exposed to any form of risk (certainly up to the cut-off point for protection under the bank deposit protection scheme). The FSA had to determine whether this product should be treated as an investment management agreement rather than as a bank deposit. From IBB's perspective, there was a substantial preference for the product to be treated as a bank deposit as it would more sensibly complement the other products in IBB's launch range of banking services. For such an instrument to be treated as a bank deposit, the FSA insisted that it must have the characteristics of a bank deposit as they are defined in subordinate legislation under the FSMA.

Article 5 of the Financial Services and Markets Act 2000 (Regulated Activities) Order 2001 (as amended) states, in paragraph 2 that:

> ... 'deposit' means a sum of money ... paid on terms
>
> (a) under which it will be repaid, with or without interest or premium, and either on demand or at a time or in circumstances agreed by or on behalf of the person making the payment and the person receiving it ...

The unconditional nature of the repayment obligation is a key feature of what constitutes a bank deposit in the United Kingdom. Conditionality through risk sharing is key to the *Sharia'a* notion of a deposit. IBB's terms for deposit accounts contain a provision (Paragraph 6) which successfully synthesises the FSA position on what properly constitutes a bank deposit and the position adopted by *Sharia'a* scholars on the pure nature of such a saving arrangement. Paragraph 6 (in full) reads as follows.

> 6.1: It is a Sharia'a principle that profit and loss sharing accounts such as the savings and term deposit account involve (1) the potential for your capital to make a profit for you and (2) the risk that your capital could suffer loss in the event of the pooled funds administered by us returning a loss.
>
> 6.2: When your capital makes a profit we shall account to you for that profit in accordance with these special conditions.
>
> 6.3: As a matter of English law (which applies to these special conditions) and in accordance with our

Memorandum and Articles of Association, in the event that your capital suffers a loss, we shall seek to mitigate the loss in the following manner:

6.3.1: we may forego some or all of the fees chargeable by us in respect of the investment of the pooled funds for the calculation period relevant to your account(s).

6.3.2: we shall draw upon any available balance in the profit stabilisation reserve account administered by us to make good as much of your capital loss as the available balance permits us to do.

6.3.3: in accordance with our Memorandum and Articles of Association, our directors are prevented from declaring any distribution to our shareholders unless they are satisfied that there is no shortfall in meeting your claim(s).

6.4: If the pooled funds referable to your capital return a loss, we shall make an offer to you to make good the amount of any shortfall that you may have suffered. We are required by current UK bank regulations and policy to make this offer to you. If you choose to accept this offer, you shall be entitled to receive payment from us of the full amount that you had previously deposited with us. You are entitled to refuse this offer from us.

6.5: We would like to draw your attention to the guidance offered by our Sharia'a Supervisory Committee. Their guidance is that if you accept our offer to make good the amount of any shortfall (set out in special condition 6.4), you will not be complying with Sharia'a principles.

6.6: In certain circumstances we may not be able to pay back to you the amount that we are obliged under these terms and conditions to pay back to you. If the terms of the Financial Services Compensation Scheme (FSCS) apply in these circumstances you may be able to apply to the FSCS for payment of compensation.

6.7: If you have suffered a loss in respect of which we have made an offer to you which you have accepted (see special condition 6.4), you may be able to apply successfully to the FSCS for payment of compensation if we fail to make payment to you in respect of that loss. If you have refused such an offer from us, you may not be able to apply successfully to the FSCS for payment of compensation in respect of the amount that was previously refused by you.

6.8: Should you suffer a capital loss due to fraud, gross misconduct or gross negligence committed by us, then we may be obliged, in accordance with Sharia'a principles, to make good to you any such capital loss on your savings or term deposit account out of money held by us on behalf of our shareholders.

Source: IBB

3. *Sharia'a* compliance and the role of the *Sharia'a* Supervisory Board

The FSA is a financial regulator, not a religious one, and it is not responsible for ensuring that a product offered is compliant with *Sharia'a* law.

Islamic banks must establish clear policies on *Sharia'a* compliance and its independent monitoring. Usually, both internal and external auditors are involved in monitoring *Sharia'a* compliance. However, UK accountants are not generally expected to be *Sharia'a* experts. It is therefore practical to appoint internal auditors who have a good grounding in Islamic law to monitor *Sharia'a* compliance.

The FSA also had to obtain an understanding of the *Sharia'a* supervisory board's role in an Islamic bank from both financial and operational perspectives. If the *Sharia'a* supervisory board's role corresponded to that of a director in a conventional bank, the individuals on the board would have to be approved by the FSA.

Sharia'a-compliant accounting practices.   The FSA attaches considerable importance to the integrity of accounting practices within financial institutions, the timely provision of management information within financial institutions and the cooperation of an institution's management with its external auditors on those occasions where external auditors are seeking to understand the nature of the company in question. From the outset, the promoters of IBB informed the FSA that *Sharia'a*-compliant accounting practices would have to be used in order to ensure product integrity from a *Sharia'a* perspective. If a product, from a *Sharia'a* perspective, entails risk sharing by the customer and by the bank, the accounting must reflect that.

The role of the Sharia'a supervisory board.   The Islamic financial institution's board of *Sharia'a* scholars is something of a curiosity for many observers. *Sharia'a* boards have policies and procedures, undertake formal meetings and will produce written notes of relevant parts of their proceeds. Such boards are as likely to meet outside the United Kingdom as they are inside it. The *Sharia'a* board has the right to seek views from whomsoever it sees fit and to ask questions of a bank's management and directors. There is an informality and flexibility around *Sharia'a* board proceedings that is attractive to the FSA. Provided that a bank's management ensures that the proceedings are suitably documented and, when an issue emerges, the resolution of it is properly documented, it appears to be the case that the burden of running a *Sharia'a* board falls upon a bank's management, as opposed to anyone else. The members of a *Sharia'a* board will be well-versed in *Sharia'a* law. *Sharia'a* scholars cover many different issues under Islamic law, which, inevitably, makes a number of them more generalised in nature than is the case with specialist finance lawyers practising within other legal jurisdictions.

4. Regulation of Islamic products

The FSA did not consider it necessary to regulate Islamic products on the wholesale market (on which historically much activity has focused in the United Kingdom). Thus, Islamic instruments traded on the wholesale markets, such as *Sukuk* and *Murabaha* contracts, were not regulated in the United Kingdom. However, the banks which traded Islamic instruments were regulated.

Whether Islamic products are sold by Islamic or conventional banks, the FSA generally does not wish to intervene on the market unless there is a market failure or if one party (usually the firm) has much more information than the other (the consumer).

5. Corporate governance issues

The FSA identified some serious and largely unresolved corporate governance issues within the 'classic' Islamic bank model.

The first issue is that Islamic banks wish to provide a steady state of return to their 'investment account holders' – that is profit and loss sharing savers – by creating reserves to smooth fluctuations, and such reserves are placed in profit equalisation accounts or investment reserve accounts. But such accounts create an inherent conflict by favouring one class of investor over another – for example, investment account holders over shareholders, or present investment account holders over future investment account holders – unless there are tight, unambiguous and prescriptive rules as regards the amounts to be placed into such accounts.

The second issue is the treatment of investment account holders within the corporate governance structure.

Investment account holders share the fortunes of the bank in a way that the traditional depositor does not. Despite this right, investment account holders do not have an automatic right to representation in the corporate governance structure. Shareholders consider that investment account holders should not be entitled to influence how the business is run or its strategic direction. However, investment account holders are vulnerable to a range of risks, such as:

- insider dealing (an employee of the bank obtains information as regards a bad loan that may result in a loss to the investment account holders);
- investment account holders earn their return on the date of the calculation of such return, and in the event that returns are diverted into or out of profit equalisation accounts to smooth fluctuations, investment account holders may actually be gaining or losing at the expense of past or future investment account holders.

These risks also arise within the securities and mutual fund industries. However, they are well understood by market players, and regulations are in place, for example, to prevent insider dealing. To date, no such regulation has been implemented in the Islamic banking industry.

Overall, the prudential Basel framework is helpful in understanding and mitigating the risks arising in Islamic banking, but the framework is insufficient, and investment account holders are best protected by means of securities-type regulations. The FSA stresses that Islamic banks should themselves recognise these risks and establish internal policies to deal with such conflicts. Islamic banks should consider instituting a corporate governance structure that embeds protection of investment account holders.

The conflicts raised by the FSA must be openly aired and understood at the level of the board of directors, and the board must set a clear and detailed framework for resolving them.

Composition of the board of directors

Given that corporate governance structures are generally designed to protect shareholders' interests, should the board have an independent member to protect the interests of the investment account holders? In the case of IBB, the FSA did not impose a disclosure regime for the protection of the investment account holders, nor has it insisted on the appointment of an independent board member to protect the interests of investment account holders. However, IBB has structured its Islamic savings products to ensure that it is *capital certain*.

The FSA's concern with respect to the board of directors is to ensure a sufficient number of independent non-executive directors with relevant financial services experience. In the IBB's case, the FSA was concerned that the independent non-executive directors should have UK retail banking experience. Experience of a *Sharia'a*-compliant institution was a much less vital consideration for the FSA. This is partly explained by understanding the role that the *Sharia'a* committee within any financial institution that wishes to be *Sharia'a*-compliant or to have an Islamic window must adopt. The IBB, naturally enough, has a *Sharia'a* committee comprising three scholars. In addition to the focus on having independent non-executive directors (at least two is the minimum stipulation), the FSA was concerned with understanding the antecedents of every other director.

Each of the other directors was seen as being affiliated in one of two ways. Either (a) the director is a member of the executive management team or (b) is a director because a major shareholder has a wish to see that person be on the board of directors. At this stage, it becomes readily apparent that the executive management team has to have conviction and confidence if it is to lead the company forward when, on the board, there may be individuals who have a substantially different perspective on the bank and its future.

Ownership issues — role of the controller

The FSMA provides that anyone who holds 10% or more of an entity that is, or wishes to be, authorised by the FSA will be treated as a controller of that entity. The FSA is entitled to approve, or disapprove, of a person or connected persons who constitute a controller. This becomes an important consideration when financing a start-up operation. Parties who are interested in financing such a project may have no interest in succumbing to the due diligence requirements that are all part of being a controller.

In the case of IBB, this was an important consideration. Potential investors were fully informed that in contributing to the pre-authorisation financing of IBB, it was possible that IBB would not be successful in its quest to obtain a banking licence from the FSA. In such circumstances, it would be highly likely that such investors would see no return on their investment and might receive back less than they had invested. To then have to submit to the due diligence requirements associated with controller status would be unattractive for many such investors.

The promoters of IBB in the pre-authorisation phase, needing to finance the costs of progressing the project to the point where it obtained FSA authorisation, carried out a private placement of shares in IBB, largely in the Middle East, in order to raise pre-FSA authorisation financing for IBB. They were successful in raising the amount that they judged necessary to take the project to the next stage: applying for, and being successful in obtaining, FSA authorisation for IBB and its business plan. In carrying out the private placement, the promoters of IBB were conscious that enthusiastic investors should be advised of the controller requirement and, in addition, investors needed to understand the nature of connected party provisions that could deem more than one person to be constituting a controller when deemed to be acting in concert with other parties. In IBB's case, a small number of investors were prepared to assume the mantle of controller status. Otherwise, a substantial body of small shareholders was created through a Middle East private placement.

When the FSA, in 2004, was wrapping up its consideration of IBB's authorisation application, it was fully aware that, following the granting of authorisation, IBB would move forward rapidly with a second capital raising and seek admission to the Alternative Investment Market (AIM) operated by the London Stock Exchange. This second capital raising was completed in October 2004.

The IBB now offers a range of retail and business banking services. It has established eight branches in cities with large Muslim populations, around the United Kingdom. According to recent figures, the bank had over 50,000 accounts and some 42,000 customers.

Islamic Financial Products Offered by the IBB

Banking with Sharia'a principles

The principles of *Sharia'a* prohibit the charging or receiving of interest. Therefore, all IBB's accounts are founded on a mutually agreed sharing of profit. Instead of charging or paying the customer interest, IBB undertakes only *Sharia'a*-compliant financing and investments. Depending on the type of account the customer holds with IBB, the IBB shares profits with them.

As a standalone bank, IBB makes every effort to ensure that IBB does not compromise on the principles of the Islamic faith. IBB never deals in products associated with alcohol, tobacco, gold or silver, nor does IBB mix IBB's funds with interest-bearing funds. The products offered include the following:

1. Current account
Pay no interest, receive no interest!

The IBB *Sharia'a*-compliant current account takes care of the essentials, offering banking services the customer would expect from a high street bank without compromising the customers' principles. The IBB current account pays the customer no interest and the customers pay no interest to the IBB.

IBB uses the Islamic principle of *Qard* for their current accounts. A *Qard* is a loan, free of profit. In essence, it means that the customer's current account is a loan to the bank, which is used by the bank for investment and other purposes. Obviously, it has to be paid back to the customer, in full, on demand.

This allows the customers peace of mind when depositing their money in a bank, with the additional reassurance that IBB is not investing their money in activities that contravene *Sharia'a* principles.

Like all IBB accounts, it has been approved by the IBB *Sharia'a* Supervisory Committee.

Current account – features and benefits

The current account is offered with a chequebook and multifunctional bank card, allowing the customers to withdraw and spend money at their convenience. Facilities offered include:

- interest-free bank account: receive no interest, pay no interest;
- debit card and cheque book with £50 cheque guarantee facility (or cash card – subject to status);
- deposits may be made by cash, cheque or direct account transfer;
- right to withdraw funds at IBB branches through an ATM, or by direct account transfer to another bank account;
- funds deposited will be administered in accordance with *Sharia'a* principles;
- standing order and direct debit facilities;
- regular statements are provided (frequency is subject to the account type);
- international payments are available;
- access to IBB foreign currency and travellers cheque services;
- automatic access to the customer's account via IBB automated telephone banking service 24/7 or online.

2. Islamic savings account

The IBB savings account is run according to the Islamic financial principles of *Mudaraba*. IBB uses the customers' money to generate a profit which will then be shared with the customer according to the Profit Sharing Ratio on the customer account.

So, the more profit IBB make with the customer's money the more the customer gets in return. Every month IBB announces its target rates for each of its savings accounts. This information is available in the IBB branches, on the IBB website and via the IBB telephone banking service. IBB normally achieves the target rates they have advertised. Some recent rates are illustrated in Table 5.1.

IBB *Sharia'a*-compliant savings account lets the customers profit from their savings while remaining true to Islamic principles. IBB does not offer the customers interest on their funds; instead, IBB undertakes *Sharia'a*-compliant activities

Table 5.1: Savings rate for the month of October 2008

Product	Target rate (%)	Achieved rate (%)
Undetermined term: the Savings Account	2.00	2.20
Young Persons Savings Account	2.50	2.50
Direct Savings Account	3.00	3.00
Fixed Term Deposit 30 days (1 month)	3.25	3.25
Fixed Term Deposit from 90 to 180 days	3.50	3.50
Fixed Term Deposit minimum 180 days (6 months)	3.75	3.75

Source: IBB

with the intention of generating profit, which, IBB then shares with the customers.

In addition to being in accordance with *Sharia'a*, IBB savings account offers complete transparency with bank charges, and the customer may make cash withdrawals from the customer's account at any of IBB branches without penalty and with no notice required. IBB's aim is to offer the customer a fair deal.

The IBB savings account is operated under *Mudaraba* principles.

What is Mudaraba?

Mudaraba refers to an investment on behalf of the customer by a more professional investor. It takes the form of a contract between two parties, one who provides the funds and the other who provides the expertise and agrees to the division of any profits made in advance. In other words, the IBB would make *Sharia'a*-compliant investments and share the profits with the customer, in effect charging for the time and effort. If no profit is made, the loss is borne by the customer and the IBB takes no fee.

Profit rates

While IBB investment methods are strictly in keeping with *Sharia'a*, IBB makes every effort to ensure that the profit rates paid on all IBB savings accounts are market competitive.

For savings accounts, the customer's share of profit is paid on the calculation date and for term deposit accounts on the maturity date of that deposit.

The following deductions are made in calculating the customer's share of profit for a calculation period:

1. **Operating fees and expenses**[1]
   The direct costs, fees and expenses are limited to 1.5% of the average pooled funds during the calculation period.
2. **Profit stabilisation reserve contribution**[1]
   The deduction from net income for a profit stabilisation reserve contribution is limited to 20% of the net income.
3. **IBB share of profit**[1]
   An illustration of the percentage of distributable profit that will be the IBB share of profit, for a calculation period, is shown in Table 5.2.

3. *Halal* Personal Finance

IBB *Halal* Personal Finance facility is an unsecured cash generating facility that allows the customer to generate cash for the purpose of purchasing goods or services, for example:

---

[1]These percentages are maximum figures and the IBB may reduce its share of profit, operating fees and expenses and the profit stabilisation reserve contribution at its discretion.

- buying a car
- refinancing a conventional loan
- holidays
- home improvements
- paying for a wedding.

The customer may apply for a *Halal* Personal Finance facility for a minimum of £5,000 up to a maximum of £25,000 and have a choice of repayment periods.

There are two rates available for Unsecured Personal Finance, one for home owners and one for non-home owners. IBB is the first fully *Sharia'a*-compliant bank to offer this facility. Finance is not secured. It is still unsecured. However, IBB is able to offer preferential rates to home owners.

Table 5.2: IBB savings accounts

Savings accounts	IBB share of distributable profit as at 2008[a] (%)
Undetermined term the 'savings account'	50.0
Young Persons Savings account	50.0
Direct Savings account	40.0
Term deposit accounts	
1 month – minimum 30 days, less than 90 days	45.0
3 months – minimum 90 days, less than 180 days	42.5
6 months – minimum 180 days	40.0

[a]These percentages are maximum figures and the IBB may reduce its share of profit, operating fees and expenses and the profit stabilisation reserve contribution at its discretion.

Like all IBB accounts, this *Halal* facility has been approved by the IBB *Sharia'a* Supervisory Committee. The *Halal* Personal

Finance facility is based on the Islamic principle of *Murabaha*. IBB buys and sells commodities and generates profit from these transactions. IBB does not charge interest, nor do the customers pay interest to IBB.

How does IBB generate cash for the Halal Personal Finance Facility?

The process of generating cash for the customer through the IBB *Halal* Personal Finance facility is, for example, as follows for a home owner facility of £10,000 over 12 months. See Box 5.1 for illustration of the mechanics. Typical annual percentage rate (APR) is 8.9% (APR is based on the profit IBB makes on the transaction, and can be used by customers for comparison purposes).

Power of Attorney

As the customer is not present during the commodity transaction, the customer gives an employee of the IBB a restricted Power of Attorney to agree to purchase the commodity on their behalf.

The customer will also sign an agency agreement appointing a broker to sell the commodity on their behalf.

In relation to the commodity transactions, both the purchase and the sale will be carried out on the same day to minimise the risk of price movement.

Membership of the Financial Services Compensation Scheme

Islamic Bank of Britain PLC is a member of the Financial Services Compensation Scheme. The scheme may provide compensation if IBB cannot meet its obligations. For example,

---

BOX 5.1 IBB personal finance facility

Step One

Customer requires £10,000 for 12 months.

Step Two

Customer enters into agreement to buy a commodity from the IBB on an agreed deferred payment period of 12 months.

Step Three

IBB sells the commodity to the customer at cost plus profit to be paid over the agreed period of time.

Step Four

Once in possession of the title to the commodity the customer appoints a third-party broker to sell the commodity on their behalf.

Step Five

The proceeds from the sale of the commodity are credited to the customer's account. The quantity of the commodity used in this transaction would enable the customer to generate the cash required.

Step Six

Customer has available funds of £10,000.

Step Seven

Customer makes monthly repayments.

Source: IBB

---

with respect to deposits with a UK office, payments under the scheme are limited to 100% of the first £2,000 of a depositor's total deposits with the bank and 90% of the next £33,000, resulting in a maximum payment of £31,700.

Most depositors, including individuals and small firms, are covered. The scheme covers deposits made with the offices of the bank within the European Union Economic Area.

Halal home finance

IBB have teamed up with the Arab Banking Corporation (ABC) to introduce customers to Alburaq Home Finance. This relationship has been approved by the IBB *Sharia'a* Supervisory Committee, who are satisfied that the technical resources complement IBB's expertise in bringing to their customers *Halal* financial products and services.

How does it work?

The *Sharia'a*-compliant home finance is based on the accepted and widely used Islamic financing principles of *Ijara* (leasing) and *Musharaka* (partnership). For example, a bank may contribute 90% and the customer 10% of the purchase price. Over a period of up to 25 years, the customer will make monthly purchase instalments through which the bank will sell its share (90%) of the home to the customer. With each instalment paid, the bank's share in the property diminishes while the customer's share correspondingly increases.

IBB stresses that they are acting as introducers only, and no advice or recommendations will be given.

How Does IBB Ensure Its Products Are Sharia'a-Compliant?

IBB's *Sharia'a* Supervisory Committee has sole responsibility when deciding on matters relating to *Sharia'a* compliancy. It is comprised of world-renowned scholars who are experts in the interpretation of Islamic law and its application in modern-day finance. They ensure that *Sharia'a* compliance is at the heart of everything IBB does.

The members of the IBB Sharia'a Supervisory Board

Sheikh Dr Abdul Sattar Abu Ghuddah, Chairman of the *Sharia'a* Supervisory Board

Sheikh Dr Abdul Sattar Abu Ghuddah is one of the world's leading scholars in the field of Islamic finance. He holds a Ph D in Islamic Law from Al Azhar University, Cairo, Egypt.

Dr Abdul Sattar has taught at various institutes, including the Imam Al Da'awa Institute in Riyadh, the Religious Institute in Kuwait and the *Sharia'a* College and Law faculty at Kuwait University. He is the Secretary General of the Unified *Sharia'a* Supervisory Board of Dallah Albaraka Group in Jeddah, a member of the Islamic Fiqh Council in Jeddah and a member of the Accounting and Auditing Organization for Islamic Financial Institutions (AAOIFI) *Sharia'a* board.

Sheikh Nizam Muhammed Seleh Yaqoobi

Sheikh Nizam is a member of a number of *Sharia'a* Supervisory Boards including the Dow Jones Islamic Index, Bahrain Islamic Bank and the Citi Islamic Investment Bank. He is also a member of the AAOIFI *Sharia'a* board and has been a visiting lecturer at Harvard University. He sits on a number of *Sharia'a* boards of other institutions.

Mufti Abdul Qadir Barkatulla

Mufti Barkatulla is a prominent *Sharia'a* scholar with a strong background in economics and finance. He is a member of the *Sharia'a* Supervisory Committees of several Islamic financial institutions including United National Bank, Alburaq of Arab Banking Corporation, London and Lloyds TSB. He is also a senior Imam of Finchley Masjid in London.

Previous Sharia'a Supervisory Board member

Sheikh Muhammad Taqi Usmani
Sheikh Muhammad Taqi Usmani was a member of the *Sharia'a* Cassation Board at the Supreme Court in Pakistan from 1982 to 2002; has been Vice President of Dar Al Uloom University, Karachi since 1974; Chairman of Islamic Economy Centre in Pakistan; Chairman of *Sharia'a* Board of AAOIFI and sits on a number of *Sharia'a* boards of other institutions.

The Sharia'a board's role

The *Sharia'a* Supervisory Board is comprised of experts in the interpretation of *Sharia'a* law and its application in modern-day Islamic financial institutions. They are world-leading scholars representing a wide spectrum of the Islamic faith and they ensure that *Sharia'a* compliance is at the heart of everything IBB does and every product and service that IBB offers.

The board meets on a regular basis to review all contracts and agreements relating to IBB transactions as well as to advise IBB, guide IBB and sanction any new services that IBB introduces.

The board certifies every account and service IBB provides. Without their approval, IBB cannot introduce a new product or service.

Sharia'a approval — certificates of endorsement (fatawa)

All of IBB products and services have the approval of their *Sharia'a* Supervisory Board and *fatawa* have been issued. These include *fatawa* for the following products:

- Current Account certificate
- Treasury Deposit Account certificate
- Master *Murabaha* certificate
- Commercial Property Finance certificate
- Personal Finance certificate
- Savings and Term Deposit certificate
- Secured Business Finance certificate
- Unsecured Business Finance certificate
- Young Persons Savings certificate
- Direct Savings Account certificate.

Appendix

Income statement

For the year ended 31 December 2006

	2006 ($)	2005 ($)
Income receivable from:		
Islamic financing transactions	4,554,578	2,985,143
Returns payable to customers and banks	(1,705,389)	(814,978)
Net income from Islamic financing transactions	(2,849,189)	(2,170,165)
Fee and commission income	174,554	40,963
Fee and commission expense	(12,764)	(3,167)
Net fee and commission income	161,790	37,796
Operating income	3,010,979	2,207,961
Net impairment loss on financial assets	(445,089)	(52,068)
Personnel expenses	(4,241,778)	(3,250,576)
General and administrative expenses	(5,430,902)	(3,859,216)
Depreciation	(621,462)	(754,689)
Amortisation	(1,105,001)	(740,919)
Total operating expenses	(11,844,232)	(8,657,468)
Loss before income tax	(8,833,253)	(6,449,507)
Income tax expense	–	–
Loss for the year	(8,833,253)	(6,449,507)
Loss per ordinary share (basic and diluted) – pence	(2.1)	(1.5)

Balance sheet

As at 31 December 2006

	2006 ($)	2005 ($)
Assets		
Cash	451,492	579,251
Commodity *Murabaha* and *Wakala* receivables and other advances to banks	100,286,964	78,037,676
Consumer finance accounts and other advances to customers	8,092,326	4,454,369
Net investment in commercial property finance	2,338,401	–
Property and equipment	3,965,370	3,798,951
Intangible assets	1,894,272	1,509,005
Other assets	983,270	910,248
Total assets	118,012,095	89,289,500
Liabilities and equity		
Liabilities		
Deposits from banks	240,164	
Deposits from customers	83,853,383	47,714,593
Other liabilities	2,187,261	1,010,367
Total liabilities	86,280,808	48,724,960
Equity		
Called up share capital	4,190,000	4,190,000
Share premium	48,747,255	48,747,255
Retained deficit	(21,205,968)	(12,372,715)
Total equity	31,731,287	40,564,540
Total equity and liabilities	118,012,095	89,289,500

Source: http://www.islamic-bank.com/islamicbanklive/FinancialCalendar/1/Home/1/Home.jsp

Chapter 6

Islamic Banking and Finance Qualifications

Introduction

There is a bewildering array of qualifications available for anyone, wishing to gain a qualification in Islamic banking and finance, but not wanting to study full time at a University or College. These qualifications differ in terms of price, content, length, quality, training methodologies, assessment systems and so on. The courses cover a wide variety of student needs.

This course summary is designed to provide answers to the FAQs about course content, duration and mode of delivery for the variety of courses available. A comprehensive summary of all the recognised courses available, including contact details, is provided. This course information is subject to change.

Readers are advised to go to the websites of the individual course providers and ensure that they provide the course which best meets individual requirements.

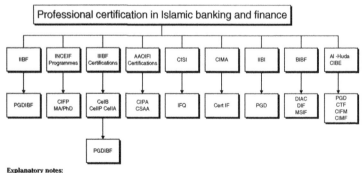

Explanatory notes:

1. IIBF: Institute of Islamic Banking and Finance

PGD: Post Graduate Diploma in Islamic Banking and Finance awarded upon completion of a 12 month Distance Learning Programme.

2. INCEIF: International Centre for Education in Islamic Finance:

CIFP: Chartered Islamic Finance Professional.

3. IIIBF: International Institute of Islamic Business and Finance.

CeIB: Certified Islamic Banker.

CeIIP: Certified Islamic Insurance Professional.

CeIIA: Certified Islamic Investment Analyst.

4. AAOIFI: Accounting and Auditing Organization for Islamic Financial Institutions

CIPA: Certified Islamic Public Accountant.

CSAA: Certified Sharia'adviser and Auditor.

5. CISI: Chartered Institute for Securities and Investment

IFQ: Islamic Finance Qualification.

6. CIMA: Chartered Institute of Management Accountants.

Cert IF: Certificate in Islamic Finance.

7. IIBI: Institute of Islamic Banking and Insurance

Post Graduate Diploma in Islamic Banking and Finance upon completion of a 12 month Distance Learning Programme.

8. BIBF: Bahrain Institute for Banking and Finance.

DIAC: Diploma in Islamic Accounting and Finance.

DIF: Diploma in Islamic Finance.

MSIF: Masters in Islamic Finance.

9. Al Huda Centre of Islamic Banking and Economics (Al Huda CIBE)

PGD: Diploma in Islamic Banking and Economics

CTF: Certified Takaful Professional

CIFM: Certified Islamic Fund Manager

CIMF:Certificate in Islamic Micro- Finance

Please note that the professional certifications listed above are in general non-statutory and non-mandatory for people engaged in Islamic finance-related practices. However, they do offer an excellent learning framework for those aspiring for a professional career in this rapidly growing industry.

Major academic and professional institutions offering diploma, undergraduate and postgraduate qualifications in Islamic banking and finance

- Association of International Accountants (AIA), UK
- Bahrain Institute of Banking and Finance (BIBF), Bahrain
- Center for Islamic Economics, Karachi, Pakistan
- Chartered Institute of Insurance, UK
- Chartered Institute for Securities and Investment
- Chartered Institute of Management Accountants, UK
- Durham University, Durham, UK
- Emirates Institute of Banking and Financial Studies, UAE
- Harvard Islamic Financing Project, Cambridge, USA

- Institute of Islamic Banking and Insurance (IIBI), London, UK
- International Islamic University Malaysia, Malaysia
- Islamic Banking and Finance Institute of Malaysia
- Islamic Research and Training Institute, IDB Jeddah, Saudi Arabia
- King Abdul Aziz University, Jeddah, Saudi Arabia
- Loughborough University, Leicester, UK
- Markfield Institute of Higher Education, Leicester, UK
- University of Bahrain.

1. Institute of Islamic Banking and Finance (IIBF)

The Institute of Islamic Banking and Finance (IIBF), incorporated with the Government of Andhra Pradesh at Hyderabad, India, is the country's maiden effort at institutionalising education at all levels in the field of Islamic economics, banking and finance. The institute is a registered non-profit, equal opportunity, professional educational research and training institution. It is totally independent and is not affiliated to any University. This principle has been established in order to retain complete academic autonomy and intellectual independence regarding course content, methodology and orientation.

Contact details: www.iibf.org.in.

Postgraduate Diploma in Islamic Banking and Finance

| **Module I** | Chapter 1 | Religious perspective – background with socio-ethical aspects of Islamic economics, banking and finance |
| | Chapter 2 | Principles and practice of Islamic financing |

Module II	Chapter 1	Islamic economics
	Chapter 2	Conventional economics
	Chapter 3	Distributive justice in Islam
	Chapter 4	*Fiqh* – Islamic financial jurisprudence
	Chapter 5	Profit versus bank interest
Module III	Chapter 1	Monetary policy from an Islamic perspective
	Chapter 2	Major problems being faced by Islamic banks
	Chapter 3	Islamic economics, banking and finance
	Chapter 4	Islamic banking and finance in theory and practice
	Chapter 5	Islamic financial institutions (IFIs) in India – historical background, present status and future strategy
	Chapter 6	Compendium of *Fatawa*s prohibiting bank interest
	Chapter 7	Resolutions, recommendations of *Al Baraka's* Symposia on Islamic Economics
Module IV	Chapter 1	Public finance in Islam – study of *Zakat*, *Ushr* and *Kharaj*
	Chapter 2	Islamic finance from a tax perspective
	Chapter 3	*Takaful* – Islamic insurance
	Chapter 4	Islamic fund management and securities markets
	Chapter 5	Islamic credit cards
Module V	This module is based on a dual learning mode that is partly in text form and partly from a CD as an e-session	

2. International Centre for Education in Islamic Finance (INCEIF)

The establishment of the International Centre for Education in Islamic Finance (INCEIF) by Bank Negara Malaysia, the central bank of Malaysia, in March 2006 represents a major investment in human capital by the government of Malaysia. INCEIF is designed to support global development of the Islamic financial industry.

Contact details: www.Inceif.org

Chartered Islamic Finance Professional (CIFP)

The CIFP programme is aimed at producing high-calibre professionals with the necessary technical skills and knowledge in Islamic finance, specifically in the areas of Islamic banking and *Takaful*.

The programme brings together industry specialists and renowned scholars in order to provide candidates with a highly qualified teaching faculty and to ensure a holistic balance between academic learning and industrial practical experience.

The programme is divided into three parts, each part offering comprehensive course modules that are designed to strategically prepare candidates to build knowledge, skills, competencies and experience as they enter the Islamic finance industry.

Candidates may apply to study at the INCEIF campus or take up the programme through distance learning.

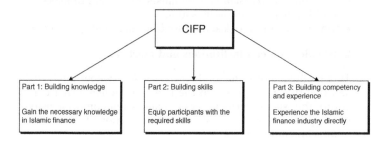

Part 1: Building knowledge

Before being conferred as associate member, candidates will be validated through examinations, written case studies and project papers based on the following modules:

1. Islamic economics and finance: theory and ethics
2. Islamic financial institutions (IFIs) and markets
3. Islamic finance regulations and governance
4. Applied *Sharia'a* in financial transactions
5. Deposit mobilisation and financial management
6. Wealth planning and management

1. Islamic economics and finance: theory and ethics

This module aims to provide students with a critical under-standing of Islamic economics by considering the implications of the application of *Sharia'a* law for the economic and financial systems.

In this module students will learn the following:

- scope of Islamic economics and finance in relation to conventional economics and finance
- history of the Islamic economic system in various eras
- contributions by Islamic economists or Muslim thinkers
- wealth creation and mobilisation
- concept of money, risk and return from an Islamic perspective.

2. Islamic financial institutions and markets

This module allows the student to develop deeper analytical and theoretical insights into the main components that constitute the Islamic financial system and a full comprehension of the various financial systems and institutions that operate in Muslim countries.

Topics include

- the functions of financial institutions and markets

- an overview of the global financial system
- the history and development of IFIs
- the Islamic financial systems of selected Muslim countries
- the IFIs (covering history and organisation, function and product and services)
- the similarities and differences of IFIs in selected Muslim countries
- Islamic financial markets (covering function and organisation, mechanism, regulators and regulations and development)
- the monetary authority/central bank.

3. Islamic finance regulations and governance

This module equips the student with a comprehensive understanding of the Islamic laws and principles that govern the Islamic financial system as well as the Islamic corporate governance mechanism that ensures the compliance of Islamic banks with the stated laws and principles.

Topics include

- an overview of regulations and governing bodies of the conventional financial system
- understanding of Islamic finance law
- source of Islamic finance law
- *Sharia'a* principles in Islamic finance
- application of *Sharia'a* principles in Islamic finance
- *Sharia'a* boards
- *Fatawa* in Islamic finance
- laws governing the Islamic financial system
- law relating to Islamic banks
- intervention by the regulatory authority.

4. Applied *Sharia'a* in financial transactions

This module provides students the opportunity to study the application and mechanism of the most widely used *Sharia'a* principles such as

- *Mudaraba*
- *Murabaha*
- *Bai Bithaman Ajil, Bai Muajjal*
- *Musawama*
- *Salam*
- *Istisna'a*
- *Ijara*
- *Bai al-Inah*
- *Tawarruq*
- *Arboun*
- *Hawala*
- *Kafala*
- *Wakala*
- *Wadia*
- *Ujr*
- *Rahn.*

At the end of these studies students will have developed an intellectual capacity to critically analyse the various aspects of *Sharia'a* principles related to the products and services offered by Islamic institutions.

5. Deposit mobilisation and financial management

This module looks at the mobilisation of deposits by conventional and Islamic banks as well as the determinants of costs of collecting deposits and forecasting techniques.

Topics include

- functions of deposits in the economy
- theories and principles related to deposits
- deposit mobilisation by conventional financial institutions
- deposit mobilisation by Islamic banks
- the cost of deposits
- saving determinants
- forecasting savings
- functions and roles of credit and financing in the economy

- rules and regulations relating to financing practices
- financing process
- use of financing evaluation techniques in credit management
- practice of financing
- secured and unsecured financing
- financial aspects of financing
- financing risk.

6. Wealth planning and management

The aim of this module is to expose students to the best ways of managing, investing and distributing wealth in accordance with Islamic laws. This module also discusses the issues related to wealth planning such as tax matters, relevant institutions and code of conduct for professionals involved in this industry.

Topics include

- functions of deposits in the economy
- nature and scope of wealth planning
- wealth (asset) allocation process
- investment in real estate
- investment in securities
- insurance and *Takaful*
- estate planning
- retirement planning
- taxation planning and management
- issues related to wealth planning and management.

Part 2: Building skills

Candidates develop skills in handling operational issues and Islamic financial transactions with the option to specialise in specific areas of Islamic banking and/or *Takaful*.

Subjects include

- structuring financing requirements

- issuing and managing Islamic securities
- *Sharia'a* compliance and audit
- customer relationship management and the role of technology
- issues in IFIs and markets.

Candidates may choose one of the two specialisations:

1. Specialised banking

- deposits and financing practices of Islamic banks
- managing Islamic banks
- treasury and risk management for Islamic banks
- legal aspects of deposits and financing.

2. Specialised *Takaful*

- managing *Takaful* institutions
- risk management in *Takaful*
- operational aspects of *Takaful*
- actuarial concepts and practices.

Part 3: Building competency and experience

The final part involves an articleship programme in which various activities are designed to provide candidates with practical experience in the Islamic financial services industry. These include mentor–mentee programmes at pre-approved participating IFIs.

Candidates will have to go through a validation process such as solving problems, restructuring exercises, simulation and management games, product conversion exercise, *Sharia'a* and audit compliance and interviews.

Successful completion of this module leads to the conferment of the Practising Member status to candidates.

3. International Institute of Islamic Business and Finance (IIIBF)

The International Institute of Islamic Business and Finance (IIIBF) Institute is operated by IBFNET. IBFNET is a global network of students, researchers, bankers and finance professionals interested in the field. Currently IBFNET has over 6000 members.

Contact details: www.iiu.edu.my.iiibf

IBFNET as an online global community has been in existence for over a decade. As an organisation it was incorporated in India in the year 1999. Among other things, IBFNET has sponsored the IIIBF and the Institute of Microfinance and Development (IMAD) to undertake education, training, research and publication programmes in the fields of Islamic Finance and Microfinance, respectively. IBFNET conducts regular personal contact seminars, workshops and training programmes.

The IIIBF offers the following professional certification programmes:

1. The Certified Islamic Banker (CeIB) programme provides professional certification for bankers, finance professionals and students.
2. The Certified Islamic Insurance Professional (CeIIP) programme provides professional certification for bankers, financial professionals and students who seek a career in the Islamic insurance (*Takaful*) sector.
3. The Certified Islamic Investment Analyst (CeIIA) programme provides professional certification for bankers, finance professionals and students who seek a career as fund managers, equity analysts and investment advisors in the industry.

All education and training programmes of IIIBF use the latest distance education methodologies. The programmes are fully administered through the Internet. Online learning is supplemented by personal contact seminars.

1. Certified Islamic Banker (CeIB) programme

Units offered

Unit	Unit name	Credit point
	Level I	
C.1	Sources of Islamic Financial Law	1
C.2	Islamic Law of Financial Contracts – I	1
C.3	Islamic Law of Financial Contracts – II	1
C.4	Islamic Financial System – I	1
C.5	Islamic Financial System – II	1
C.6	Islamic Monetary and Macroeconomic Management	1
	Level II	
E.1	Islamic Commercial Banking: Products and Services	1
E.2	Islamic Commercial Banking: Operations and Management	1
E.3	Islamic Microfinance	1
E.4	Islamic Investment Banking	1
E.5	Project Appraisal and Investment Decisions	1
E.6	Accounting Standards and Regulations for Islamic Banks	1

Unit	Unit name	Credit point
E.7	Information Technology for Islamic Financial Institutions	1
E.8	Marketing of Islamic Financial Services	1
E.9	Total Quality Management and Business Process Re-engineering for Islamic Financial Institutions	1
P.1	Supervised Project – I	1
P.2	Supervised Project – II	2

2. Certified Islamic Insurance Professional (CeIIP) programme

Course specification for CeIIP (12 credit points).

Units offered

Unit	Unit name	Credit point
Level I		
C.1	Sources of Islamic Financial Law	1
C.2	Islamic Law of Financial Contracts – I	1
C.3	Islamic Law of Financial Contracts – II	1
C.4	Islamic Financial System – I	1
C.5	Islamic Financial System – II	1
C.6	Islamic Monetary and Macroeconomic Management	1
Level II		
E.10	Islamic Insurance: Products and Services	1

Unit	Unit name	Credit point
E.12	Islamic Insurance: Operations and Management	1
E.3	Islamic Microfinance	1
E.4	Islamic Investment Banking	1
E.5	Project Appraisal and Investment Decisions	1
E.13	Accounting Standards and Regulations for Islamic Insurance Companies	1
E.7	Information Technology for Islamic Financial Institutions	1
E.8	Marketing of Islamic Financial Services	1
E.9	Total Quality Management and Business Process Re-engineering for Islamic Financial Institutions	1
P.1	Supervised Project – I	1
P.2	Supervised Project – II	2

3. Certified Islamic Investment Analyst (CeIIA) programme

Course specification for CeIIA (12 credit points)

Units offered

Unit	Unit name	Credit point
Level I		
C.1	Sources of Islamic Financial Law	1
C.2	Islamic Law of Financial Contracts – I	1
C.3	Islamic Law of Financial Contracts – II	1

Unit	Unit name	Credit point
C.4	Islamic Financial System – I	1
C.5	Islamic Financial System – II	1
C.6	Islamic Monetary and Macroeconomic Management	1
Level II		
E.13	Security Analysis and Portfolio Management	1
E.14	Capital Markets in Emerging Economies	1
E.3	Islamic Microfinance	1
E.4	Islamic Investment Banking	1
E.5	Project Appraisal and Investment Decisions	1
E.13	Accounting Standards and Regulations for Islamic Insurance Companies	1
E.7	Information Technology for Islamic Financial Institutions	1
E.8	Marketing of Islamic Financial Services	1
E.9	Total Quality Management and Business Process Re-engineering for Islamic Financial Institutions	1
P.1	Supervised Project – I	1
P.2	Supervised Project – II	2

Postgraduate Diploma in Islamic Business and Finance (PGDIBF) programme

Course specification for PGDIBF (16 credit points).

Entry requirements

To qualify for entry to the PGDIBF programme, applicants normally must have completed the 12-unit CeIB/CeIP/CeIIA programme offered by IIIBF.

Persons meeting the above requirements will be required to complete four additional credit points of approved study in order to be awarded the PGDIBF.

Normally, students must complete the units in the sequence in which they appear in the table of description of units. Level I and Level II must be completed before a student moves on to Level III.

Units offered

Unit	Unit name	Credit point
	Level III	
A.1	Principles of Islamic Business Ethics	1
A.2	Principles of Islamic Management	1
A.3	Research Gaps in Islamic Business and Finance	1
A.4	Supervised Project	1

4. Accounting and Auditing Organization for Islamic Financial Institutions (AAOIFI)

The Accounting and Auditing Organization for Islamic Financial Institutions (AAOIFI) is an Islamic international autonomous not-for-profit corporate body that prepares accounting, auditing, governance, ethics and *Sharia'a* standards for IFIs and the industry.

Contact details: www.aaoifi.org

AAOIFI was established in accordance with the Agreement of Association which was signed by IFIs on 26 February 1990 in

Algiers. AAOIFI was registered on 27 March 1991 in the State of Bahrain.

AAOIFI offers the following qualifications:

1. Certified Islamic Professional Accountant (CIPA)

Programme objectives
The Certified Islamic Professional Accountant (CIPA) programme is designed to equip candidates with the requisite technical understanding and professional accounting skills for international Islamic banks and financial institutions. Through the CIPA programme, candidates gain advanced knowledge of

- objectives and concepts of financial accounting for international Islamic banks and financial institutions;
- accounting rules for international Islamic banking and finance transactions;
- general presentation and disclosure for financial statements of international Islamic banks and financial institutions;
- application of *Sharia'a* for international Islamic banking and finance products and services;
- effective governance and *Sharia'a* compliance structures in international Islamic banks and financial institutions.

Programme content
The CIPA programme covers technical accounting subjects for international Islamic banks and financial institutions, including

- development of international Islamic banking and financial systems and functions of Islamic banks and financial institutions;
- accounting concepts and principles for international Islamic banking and finance;

- qualitative characteristics of accounting information for international Islamic banking and finance;
- AAOIFI's Accounting Standards on financial reporting for the international Islamic banking and finance industry;
- AAOIFI's *Sharia'a* Standards on Islamic finance products and practices, and the *Sharia'a* basis for those standards;
- AAOIFI's Governance Standards on *Sharia'a* compliance and a review of the processes.

Programme details

- Candidates are provided with study packages upon successful registration into the programme. A training session for candidates is held subsequent to the close of registration of each intake, and an examination is conducted at the end of the programme. Duration from the close of registration of each intake to the examination is approximately 4 months.
- Study packages for the programme include AAOIFI's Standards publications and CIPA course materials.

2. Certified Sharia'a Adviser and Auditor (CSAA)

Programme objectives

The Certified *Sharia'a* Adviser and Auditor (CSAA) programme is designed to equip candidates with the requisite technical understanding and professional skills regarding *Sharia'a* compliance and to review the processes for the international Islamic banking and finance industry. Through the CSAA programme, candidates will gain advanced knowledge of

- roles and functions of various *Sharia'a* compliance and review processes in financial institutions;

- the relationship between a financial institution's *Sharia'a* Supervisory Board (SSB) and its internal *Sharia'a* compliance and review processes;
- mechanisms to ensure *Sharia'a* compliance in accordance with resolutions and *Fatawas* (Scholars' rulings) issued by the SSB;
- technical review of banking and financial operations to determine *Sharia'a* compliance;
- the foundations necessary to gain stakeholders' trust and confidence in a financial institution's adherence to *Sharia'a*.

Programme content
The CSAA programme covers technical subjects that are essential for *Sharia'a* compliance and review processes for the international Islamic banking and finance industry, including

- AAOIFI's *Sharia'a* standards on Islamic finance products and practices, and *Sharia'a* basis for those standards;
- AAOIFI's Governance Standards on *Sharia'a* compliance and a review of the processes;
- Islamic banking and finance supervision (including regulatory and external supervision, internal review and the application of AAOIFI's standards);
- operational structures for *Sharia'a* compliance and review;
- *Sharia'a* compliance and a review of the procedures (including planning, operations, documentation and reporting);
- application of *Sharia'a* and *Fiqh* (Islamic jurisprudence) to Islamic banking and finance practices.

Programme details
- Candidates are provided with study packages upon successful registration into the programme. A training session for candidates is held subsequent to the close of

registration of each intake, and an examination is conducted at the end of the programme. Duration from the close of registration of each intake to the examination is approximately 4 months.

- Study packages for the programme include AAOIFI's standards publications and CSAA course materials.
- Training sessions are conducted by *Sharia'a* scholars and members of AAOIFI's *Sharia'a* Board.

5. Chartered Institute for Securities and Investment (CISI)

The Chartered Institute for Securities and Investment (CISI) is the largest and most widely respected professional body for those who work in the securities and investment industry in the United Kingdom and in a growing number of major financial centres round the world. Formed in 1992 by London Stock Exchange practitioners, the CISI now has more than 40,000 members in 89 countries.

Contact details: www.cisi.org.uk

The CISI is a registered charity and has the following charitable objects:

- to promote, for the public benefit, the advancement and dissemination of knowledge in the field of securities and investments;
- to develop high ethical standards for practitioners in securities and investments and to promote such standards in the United Kingdom and overseas;
- to act as an authoritative body for the purpose of consultation and research in matters of education or public interest concerning investment in securities.

CISI offers the following Islamic qualification.

Islamic Finance Qualification (IFQ)

Key features of the IFQ

- Candidates gain a basic knowledge of the general principles of the *Sharia'a* (*Fiqh* al *Mu'amalat*) and its application to Islamic banking and finance.
- Candidates acquire knowledge of the different types of Islamic finance contracts and products from both a technical and *Sharia'a* perspective.
- Candidates expand their understanding of the practices used in the Islamic financial markets and the principles behind investment selection.
- Equipping candidates with the Islamic finance qualification (IFQ) indicates that a company is willing to contribute to the development and promotion of high ethical standards of employees working in the Islamic financial services industry.
- The syllabus, workbook, other teaching materials and examinations have been developed with the support and collaboration of a panel of internationally recognised experts in Islamic finance.
- The qualification is reviewed annually to reflect developments in the fast-changing world of Islamic financial services.
- The qualification was initiated, and is supported, by the Central Bank of Lebanon (Banque du Liban).
- Staff gain a prestigious qualification from both the Chartered Institute for Securities and Investment (recognised by the UK government education regulator) and the Ecole Supérieure des Affaires, which is managed by the Paris Chamber of Commerce and Industry.
- The qualification is available internationally.

IFQ summary syllabus
Element 1: An introduction to Islam

The principles and concepts which underpin Islam; the placing of banking and finance within Islam; the sources and interpretation of Islamic law; introduction to the role of the SSB.

Element 2: An introduction to Islamic banking and finance

The basis of Islamic banking and finance; the development of the Islamic finance and banking industry; the main components of the Islamic banking industry and its operating structures.

Element 3: Islamic law of contracts

Principles of Islamic business including the avoidance of *riba* and *gharar*; the concept of *Wa'd* (promise); the elements of a valid contract; the different types of contract; the purchase and sale of currencies.

Element 4: Financial techniques applied by Islamic banks

The nature of Islamic current accounts; the nature of the major contracts – *Mudaraba, Musharaka, Murabaha, Ijara, Salam, Istisna'a*; the use of letters of credit and guarantees in Islamic finance contracts.

Element 5: Financial statements for Islamic banks

The framework of International Financial Reporting Standards (IFRS); contents of the main financial statements; the need for specific Islamic accounting standards; the role of AAOIFI and IFRS.

Element 6: Islamic corporate governance

The different approaches to corporate governance; additional challenges presented by Islamic banks; the role of the SSB and corporate governance issues in *Takaful*.

Element 7: Islamic asset and fund management

The purpose of investment in Islam; prohibited industries; replicating conventional deposit structures using *Murabaha* and *Mudaraba*; investment funds using *Ijara*; the Islamic stock selection process and the role of the SSB.

Element 8: Islamic bond market – *Sukuk*

The nature of *Sukuk* compared with conventional bonds; issuing *Sukuk*; different types of *Sukuk*; AAOIFI Standards for *Sukuk* and rating *Sukuk* issues.

Element 9: Islamic insurance – *Takaful*

The nature and structure of *Takaful* compared with conventional insurance; remunerating the insurance operator; *Sharia'a* governance of *Takaful* undertakings.

The examinations are computer based and can be taken at CISI accredited assessment centres throughout the world.

A list of CBT Testing Centres is provided in the Appendix.

6. Chartered Institute for Management Accountants (CIMA)

The Chartered Institute for Management Accountants (CIMA) is a leading membership body that offers a globally recognised professional management accounting qualification. CIMA qualifications have an emphasis on accounting for business.

Contact details: www.cimaglobal.com

CIMA is the voice of over 171,000 members and students in 165 countries. It is responsible for the education and training of management accountants who work in industry, commerce, not-for-profit and public sector organisations.

CIMA works with some of the world's leading employers and course providers around the world to educate, train and qualify first-class financial managers. CIMA prides itself on the commercial relevance of its syllabuses which are regularly updated to reflect the latest business developments and employer needs.

CIMA offers the Islamic qualification described below.

CIMA Certificate in Islamic Finance (Cert IF)

The CIMA Certificate in Islamic Finance (Cert IF) is the first global qualification to be offered by a professional chartered accountancy body and is designed to focus on the fast growing sector of Islamic finance. It is available to staff currently working within the Islamic financial services industry and to those entering the sector.

The certificate is valuable for newcomers to Islamic finance as well as financial professionals seeking accreditation and qualification in this field. It is designed to give professionals two significant market advantages:

- the professional recognition of a CIMA international qualification
- demonstrable expertise in the complex, fast growing world of Islamic finance.

What skills does Cert IF teach?
The Cert IF gives candidates comprehensive skills in key areas including *Sharia'a* compliance and the complexities of the contracts that underpin this compliance. Candidates also develop confidence in using the terminology and applying the knowledge that sets Islamic finance apart from conventional finance.

The Cert IF is an international qualification and is available for study across the globe. CIMA's aim is to give candidates a thorough knowledge of the theory that underpins Islamic finance.

Course modules

The certificate has four compulsory study modules. Each is covered by a detailed study guide that takes candidates through to the examinations.

The Cert IF is a self-study, distance learning qualification, and is available for study across the globe. Each module is independent of the other modules. CIMA recommends that candidates complete the Islamic Commercial Law module first as it includes knowledge and skills candidates will require for the three remaining modules.

CIMA estimates that it will take between 2 and 6 months to reach a stage where candidates can sit for all the final examinations, depending on prior knowledge and experience.

Study modules

The CIMA Cert IF is a self-study, distance learning qualification that allows students to progress at their own pace.

There are four compulsory modules:

1. Islamic Commercial Law
2. Banking and *Takaful*
3. Islamic Capital Markets and Instruments
4. Accounting for Islamic Financial Institutions.

Each module has a study guide, which offers

- a comprehensive syllabus leading to a higher professional qualification in Islamic finance
- step by step subject coverage directly linked to specific learning outcomes
- fusion between theory and practice
- chapter summaries
- contemporary and user-friendly glossary of Islamic finance terms
- extensive question practice

- revision sections for each chapter
- a full length mock examination at the end of each guide.

Final examination
Candidates will need to pass an electronic final assessment in all four modules to gain the certificate. Each assessment has between 40 and 50 multiple choice questions, depending on the number of assessment criteria in the module.

The examinations are computer based and can be taken at CIMA accredited assessment centres throughout the world.

A list of CBT Testing Centres is provided in the Appendix.

7. Institute of Islamic Banking and Insurance (IIBI)

The mission of the IIBI, based in London, is to be a centre of excellence for professional education, training, research and related activities and to build a wider knowledge base and deeper understanding of the world of finance, thereby promoting the Islamic principles of equity, socio-economic justice and inclusiveness. The institute is also committed to making contributions, donations and other payments to empower people to improve lives and contribute responsibly in the global community and to encourage debate on the relationship between ethics, morality and finance in such a manner as the institute shall, from time to time, direct.

Contact details: www.islamic-banking.com

Postgraduate Diploma (PGD)

The Postgraduate Diploma (PGD) course in Islamic banking and insurance is a distance learning course comprising six modules offering candidates the opportunity to study at home, and at their own pace, and to respond to questions which are given at the end of each lesson. Each module builds on the knowledge of the previous one. The questions at the end of each lesson are designed to test the understanding of the basic concepts which have been explored within the lessons. To qualify for the Institute's PGD, a student must successfully complete all six modules.

Course syllabus
Module 1: Islamic Economics and Finance

This module provides an introduction to the concepts of Islamic economics and Divine Guidance in Islam. It illustrates the characteristics of an interest-free economy based on the principles of socio-economic justice.

Lesson 1   An introduction to the concepts of Islamic economics

Lesson 2   Divine guidance for an Islamic economy

Lesson 3   Evolution of Islamic interest-free banking.

Module 2: Islamic Commercial Law and Contract

This module explains the Islamic principles and the modes used in financing and contracts, such as *Qard*, *Dayn*, *Musharaka*, *Mudaraba*, *Ijara*, *Wakala*, *Kafala*, *Hawala*, *Jua'alah* and *Tawarruq*.

Lesson 1   Islamic commercial law and the concepts, principles and forms of *Bai*' (trading).

Lesson 2   *Qard* and *Dayn* in Islamic commercial law.

Lesson 3   *Musharaka* and *Mudaraba*.

Lesson 4   Diminishing *Musharaka* as a financing mode.

Lesson 5   Credit sales: *Murabaha* and *Musawama*.

Lesson 6   Future sales: *Salam* and *Istisna'a*.

Lesson 7   *Ijara* (leasing) in Islamic finance.

Lesson 8   Accessory contracts (*Wakala*, *Kafala*, *Jua'alah*, *Tawarruq* and *Istijrar*).

Module 3: Islamic Banking Operations

This module provides an introduction to the conventional banking system and goes on to deal with the key operations of Islamic banks and cooperation between conventional and Islamic financial institutions.

Lesson 1   An outline of the conventional banking system

Lesson 2   Deposit/resource mobilisation by Islamic banks

Lesson 3   Financing by Islamic banks – asset side

Lesson 4   Islamic banks services and fee-based operations

Lesson 5   Cooperation between conventional and Islamic financial institutions.

Module 4: Treasury and Capital Market Operations

This module deals with the Islamic financial markets, scope and instruments. It also discusses the concepts of venture capital, investment funds, unit trusts, securitisation and *Sukuk*, all in accordance with Islamic principles.

Lesson 1   Islamic financial markets and instruments

Lesson 2   Venture capital under the Islamic financial system

Lesson 3   Islamic funds and unit trusts

Lesson 4   Securitisation and *Sukuk*.

Module 5: Regulation, Supervision and Corporate Governance

This module deals with governance and transparency issues in IFIs, supervisory and regulatory issues, the role of the Religious Board, *Sharia'a* compliance audit, accounting and taxation issues. It also provides guidelines for the conversion of interest-based banking to Islamic interest-free banking and the practical steps for establishing an Islamic bank.

Lesson 1   Good governance and transparency in IFIs

Lesson 2   Supervisory issues, internal controls and audit for *Sharia'a* compliance

Lesson 3   Accounting and taxation Issues in Islamic banking

Lesson 4   Islamic banks financial statements

Lesson 5   Practical steps for establishing an Islamic bank

Lesson 6   Conversion of a conventional bank to an Islamic bank.

Module 6: *Takaful* – Alternative to Insurance

This module explains *Takaful* and its rationale as an alternative to conventional insurance, the basic elements and models for *Takaful* business and *Retakaful* (Reinsurance).

Lesson 1   Concept, objective, basis and principles of *Takaful*

Lesson 2   Basic elements of *Takaful*

Lesson 3   *Takaful* business models and operational issues

Lesson 4   Family *Takaful* and areas of application

Lesson 5   General *Takaful* and areas of application

Lesson 6 *Retakaful* or reinsurance

Lesson 7 Regulatory framework in the *Takaful* industry.

8. Bahrain Institute of Banking and Finance (BIBF)

The Bahrain Institute of Banking and Finance (BIBF) is a leading professional training institute in Bahrain and the Gulf Region. It was founded in 1981 to provide essential training for the banking community in Bahrain. Since then it has evolved into an internationally recognised training and development organisation where over 100,000 students have attended courses since its inception.

Contact details: www.bibf.com

- BIBF has been recognised as a provider of superior value, uncompromising high levels of customer satisfaction and results-oriented solutions.
- BIBF has highly qualified faculty members of diverse nationalities devoted to advancing and enriching the human experience.
- BIBF has delivered quality programmes in countries around the globe including, for example, Saudi Arabia, Kuwait, Oman, United Arab Emirates, Qatar, Malaysia, Indonesia and Sudan, and it has provided instruction to participants from over 50 countries at BIBF.
- BIBF enjoys strategic relationships with internationally recognised professional organisations which deliver programmes jointly with BIBF. Among such organisations are the Federal Reserve Bank of New York, American Bankers Association, US Securities and Exchange Commission, NASDAQ, Darden Graduate School of Business (University of Virginia), DePaul University, Bentley College, University of Wales, University of Cambridge International

Examinations, **ifs** *School of Finance*, Chartered Association of Certified Accountants and the Chartered Insurance Institute.

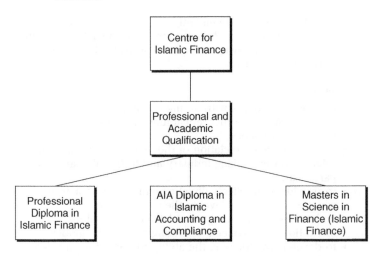

BIBF offers a variety of Islamic financial qualifications though the Centre for Islamic Finance, as given below.

Diploma in Islamic Finance (DIF)

What is the Diploma in Islamic Finance (DIF)?
The Diploma in Islamic Finance (DIF) programme is a professional qualification addressing the needs of both Islamic and conventional financial institutions providing Islamic banking services and products. It is a part-time evening programme emphasising the practical aspects of Islamic banking with broad coverage of the theoretical foundation of the subject.

The programme is structured on the semester system and requires credit hours (6 modules with 60 hours each). Participants are expected to do the required credit hours, pass their semester exams and undertake certain assignments in order to graduate. As a professional qualification the programme emphasises the current practices of Islamic banking.

The lecturers are predominantly practitioners and the study material is drawn from the practice of various IFIs. Each module comes with its own comprehensive manual authored by experts in the industry.

Objectives

- to provide students with an understanding of the jurisprudential and theoretical fundamentals of Islamic banking and finance;
- to provide an appreciation of the investment regulations relating to the banking industry and to Islamic banks in particular;
- to provide an intellectually stimulating environment in which students can develop their knowledge, understanding and analysis of Islamic financial markets, institutions and systems operating around the globe;
- to develop, in students, the ability to apply the knowledge and skills they have acquired for the solution of practical problems in their professional banking careers;
- to train executives seeking to specialise in Islamic banking and finance in order to assist expansion in the banking and finance industry.

Programme structure

The DIF programme is run flexibly in the evenings to suit the working hours of professionals, while simultaneously offering a number of sessions to give candidates the opportunity to fast track their progression. The programme is structured on a 20-week semester system and students are required to complete six modules, each having 60 in-class hours. The modules are as follows and can be completed in any order:

1. Islamic Commercial Jurisprudence
2. Introduction to Trust, Banking and Business Laws

3. Islamic Insurance (*Takaful*)
4. Islamic Treasury, Capital Markets and Risk Management
5. Islamic Banking Operations
6. Islamic Accounting Standards.

Intended learning outcomes

On successful completion of the programme, graduates should be able to demonstrate knowledge and understanding of

- the jurisprudential and theoretical foundations of Islamic banking and finance;
- the regulations (accounting) and laws (commercial, banking and trust laws) applying to banks in general and Islamic banks in particular
- the basic jurisprudential principles of Islamic Insurance; (*Takaful*) and its operational application by IFIs;
- the forms of financing instruments (retail, investment and treasury) utilised in Islamic finance and the contexts in which they are applied;
- the practical day to day operations of Islamic banks in detail;
- operations of financial markets, institutions and infrastructure within an Islamic system;
- the current issues facing IFIs and the overall Islamic finance industry.

Diploma in Islamic Accounting and Compliance (DIAC)

What is the DIAC?

The Diploma in Islamic Accounting and Compliance (DIAC) is a professional certification jointly developed and certified by the BIBF and the AIA. The DIAC programme seeks to develop the next generation of accounting professionals and leaders in Islamic finance. It is specifically designed to cater to the needs of global professionals who require a qualification that enhances and certifies their knowledge and practical understanding of the multi-jurisdictional accounting systems that Islamic banks are exposed to. The programme is divided into four modules, all of which are examined directly by the AIA in a number of locations. These modules are listed out below.

The AIA, a premier international professional accountancy body, is responsible for setting the syllabi for the course, preparing the independently developed exam papers and appointing leading professional examiners.

The BIBF is responsible for compiling the course structure and providing highly reputed teaching and support services.

Learning objectives
The learning objectives of the course are as follows:

1. to introduce candidates to Islamic commercial jurisprudence in order for them to appreciate the religious basis of the instruments and the associated financial accounting standards (FASs) utilised in IFIs;
2. to provide a detailed overview of the operational environment of IFIs, in order for graduates to appreciate the operational realities associated with the accounting transactions;
3. to engender an appreciation of the unique ethical and governance features of IFIs and the associated rules and standards;
4. to ground the conceptual basis and standards associated with accounting for IFIs;
5. to provide an insight into the complexities of multi-jurisdictional accounting standards for IFIs;
6. to assist graduates in preparing financial statements that comply with both IFRS and Islamic accounting standards.

Why study for the DIAC?

- to achieve a professional accounting certification from a world-renowned association;

- to enjoy the training resources of the Gulf's pre-eminent finance institute;
- to take the first step on a fast track into professional career opportunities in IFIs;
- to gain an unprecedented and comprehensive overview of the religious, legal and operational realities of accounting for IFIs.

Who is the DIAC designed for?
The DIAC has been designed with the following individuals in mind:

- those who plan to have a career in Islamic banks or financial institutions, particularly in financial control, product development or compliance;
- those who are already employed by an Islamic bank or financial institution but desire a globally recognised professional qualification.

Course programme
The course contains four modules, all of which are examinable. Upon passing the examinations for all four modules in the programme, candidates will be awarded a jointly certified DIAC from the AIA and the BIBF.

The four course modules are as follows:

1. Islamic Commercial Law

This module introduces candidates to the complexities of Islamic commercial jurisprudence with a focus on the juristic justifications for and particular laws applicable to each specific Islamic nominate contract utilised in Islamic finance. This module enables candidates to appreciate the Islamic juristic rules and to subsequently apply the substance of such rules in the accounting and compliance practices. An introduction to the Islamic economic paradigm is also given.

2. Islamic Banking Practice

This module provides a detailed overview of the operations of IFIs from a practical perspective. This module enables candidates to appreciate the operational realities of Islamic finance in order to produce representative accounting numbers. Topics covered range from Islamic bank operations overview, detailed coverage of the sources and uses of funds in an Islamic financial institution, bank risks and risk management mechanisms. An introduction to the Islamic infrastructure institutions is also given.

3. Islamic Accounting Standards

This module provides a detailed coverage of each FAS promulgated by the AAOIFI, with an analysis of the parallel IFRS issued by the International Accounting Standards Board (IASB), where relevant. Particular focus is given to comparative conceptual frameworks for IFRS and FAS, the accounting standards for each Islamic nominate contract, the method and disclosure of profit allocation between shareholders and investment account holders and the presentation requirements in the financial reports of IFIs. The presentation requirements for Islamic insurance companies are also covered as an optional section.

4. Auditing, Ethics and Corporate Governance

This module provides a detailed coverage of Islamic business ethics and its implications on the role of corporate governance and auditing for IFIs, including awareness of contemporary challenges related to governance and auditing practices. The module particularly focuses on the unique *Sharia'a* and investment account holder's related governance issues. The Code of Ethics for Accountants and Auditors and the Standards of Corporate Governance promulgated by the AAOIFI are utilised as a benchmark of best practice and discussed comprehensively. The module also covers the scope of auditing IFIs.

A detailed syllabus is available on the AIA website: www.aiaworldwide.com.

Masters of Science – Islamic Finance (MSIF)

Statement of DePaul University (the BIBF partner)
Over the course of the last decade, the Islamic finance segment of the financial services industry has experienced a phenomenal rate of growth. This, in turn, has created a significant demand for finance professionals who are

- equipped with a deep understanding of the nuances of the field;
- able to contribute to the design and the trading of *Sharia'a*-compliant sophisticated financial products;
- well-versed in the workings of the markets within which these activities take place.

The DePaul Master of Science-Islamic Finance, offered jointly with the Center for Islamic Finance at BIBF, builds on the strength of DePaul's Master of Science in Finance programme and the unique capabilities of the BIBF faculty. The core curriculum of this programme provides participants with a sophisticated framework for a deep understanding of arbitrage, interest rates, risk and return, fair value, value formation and other important financial theories.

The increasing sophistication of financial markets and an ever-expanding set of instruments traded within its increasingly globalised setting demand a deep understanding. Success within this market requires the mastery of an array of competencies. These include a theoretically sound and applied understanding of

- how the regional and global markets of the world evolve;

- the nature and the role of innovation within and across the markets;
- the governing mechanisms needed for the well-functioning of the markets;
- the process of innovation and its interaction within and across the markets;
- the governing mechanisms needed for the good functioning of the markets;
- the process of innovation and its interaction with regulation;
- the principles governing valuation of different forms of assets, contingent assets and derivatives;
- strategic financial decision-making;
- financial analysis;
- management of financial services firms;
- complex and tailor-made forms of financing;
- resource allocation;
- corporate governance;
- corporate restructuring.

The core curriculum is designed to provide participants with the requisite knowledge, and the know-how, to successfully tackle these issues. It is delivered by a faculty known for its dedication to teaching and well recognised for its academic accomplishments. Most members of the faculty have had significant work experience in key corporate positions prior to joining DePaul. Many are renowned scholars within their field of research and enjoy national and international reputations. They include well-published and often-cited researchers, authors of best-selling textbooks and editors of highly respected academic journals.

Building upon this foundation, the students of the programme will be provided the opportunity to acquire a deep and thorough understanding of the Islamic economic and financial systems and the workings of its markets. Once such mastery is acquired, the graduates of the programme will be in a position to contribute to the process of building and managing wealth in a *Sharia'a*-compliant manner.

Why study the Master of Science – Islamic Finance (MSIF)?
The Master of Science – Islamic Finance programme provides an opportunity for highly motivated students to develop the dual knowledge and skills base necessary to understand modern conventional and Islamic financial markets, instruments and decision-making. Complementing DePaul's existing reputation in Finance, BIBF has sourced globally recognised experts in Islamic finance to deliver the Islamic finance courses. The programme is structured to develop financial management professionals with the knowledge and proficiency to

- create sophisticated solutions to financial problems;
- structure and evaluate new financial instruments for both Islamic and conventional institutions;
- leverage resources for optimal profitability and productivity;
- develop strategic financial objectives;
- seize new business opportunities;
- mitigate corporate risk;
- improve investment decision-making;
- analyse technical financial material;
- understand the technicalities of Islamic commercial and investment banking.

MSIF programme structure
The Masters of Science – Islamic Finance (MSIF) degree is structured on the basis of two specialisations and hence includes topics to be covered in both the conventional finance stream and the Islamic finance stream. These are given below.

Seven finance courses

ECO 555 Economics for Decision Making

FIN 555 Financial Management

FIN 523 Investment Analysis

FIN 524 Financial Statement Analysis

FIN 512 Commercial Banking

FIN 562 Derivatives and Risk Management

FIN 662 Advanced Derivatives and Risk Management.

Five Islamic finance courses

Islamic Economics, Jurisprudence and Ethics

Accounting, Auditing and Governance for IFIs

Islamic Commercial Banking

Islamic Investment Banking

Islamic Treasury, Capital Markets and Risk management.

MSIF curriculum
Students complete the Master of Science – Islamic Finance by taking a total of 12 courses, as specified above.

In addition, students will be required to attend the AAOIFI Annual Conference on Islamic Banking and the AAOIFI Annual *Sharia'a* Conference held during the year.

Finance courses

ECO 555 Economics for Decision-Making

This course provides students with an opportunity to apply microeconomic principles to managerial decision-making. These principles include those underlying the theories of consumer choice, production and cost as they relate to decisions made by firms and households. Specific topics include consumer demand analysis and estimation; elasticity; production theory; cost structure and estimation; profit maximisation and the effect of market structure on pricing, output and profit.

FIN 555 Financial Management

A study of the major decision areas faced by the corporate financial manager and their relationship to the goals of the firm's owners. Specific topics include capital budgeting, capital structure and the cost of capital, dividend policy and current asset management.

FIN 523 Investment Analysis

This course provides an overview of the investment environment for the institutional money manager. The market mechanism, market equilibrium, the relationship between risk and return and the valuation of various investment instruments are investigated.

FIN 524 Financial Statement Analysis

This course develops financial analysis skills from the view of an outsider using a corporation's publicly available financial statements. Techniques such as common sizing, ratio analysis, decomposition and the use of a comprehensive DuPont Model are used as a basis to teach analytical thought processes necessary to make projections for a company based on its financial statements. The use of spreadsheets as an analytical tool will be strongly emphasised.

FIN 512 Commercial Banking

The purpose of the course is to analyse the role of commercial banks in the financial system. The present structure of banking will be studied with particular emphasis on the relationship between commercial banking practices and economic stabilisation goals. Issues in bank asset management, liability management and capital adequacy will be presented. Finally, new dimensions in banking will be considered.

FIN 562 Derivatives and Risk Management

This course is designed as an introduction to derivative instruments, their characteristics, their pricing, the market's infrastructure, trading mechanics and applications. The course introduces the binomial pricing model, the Black and Scholes continuous time pricing model, the associated properties, that is, 'the Greeks' and forward pricing. The course examines the characteristics and market infrastructure for each of the four derivative instruments: forwards, futures, options and swaps. Then trading strategies and hedging applications for each of these instruments are discussed. The course concludes with an introduction to Value at Risk.

FIN 662 Advanced Derivatives and Risk Management

This course is designed to be an advanced course that focuses on the pricing models for the four derivative instruments: forwards, futures, options and swaps. Fixed income modelling as it is related to swaps and caps also will be considered. The first part of the course is devoted to an in depth examination of the various pricing models: discrete, continuous time, as well as Monte Carlo simulation. Each model's properties are derived and discussed in detail. These models are then applied to a range of realistic pricing situations which include swaps, exotic options, credit derivatives and complex Value at Risk problems.

Islamic finance courses

Islamic Economics, Jurisprudence and Ethics

This course will introduce students to *Sharia'a* laws related to commerce and trade (*Fiqh Al-Muamalat*) and how they are applied in the international commercial environment. Students will develop an appreciation of the economics of Islamic finance as it relates to the ethical underpinnings and worldview set forth in *Sharia'a* law. Students will learn how to apply *Sharia'a* principles to financial transactions that they will encounter in IFIs. This course will also foster an appreciation of the debates on contentious issues in contemporary Islamic finance transactions.

Islamic Commercial Banking

This course will provide students with a substantial overview of the commercial banking operations of IFIs, covering three distinct areas: retail, trade and corporate banking services. In the retail aspect of the course, students will be introduced to the different Islamic products available for retail banking including deposit and financing products, credit cards and banking services. The course will focus on the structuring and operational process of the products. The course will also feature a heavy bias towards contemporary case studies drawn from a host of IFIs operating across the globe attempting to showcase innovative and original Islamic products and structures. By the end of the course, students will appreciate the dynamics of creating innovative products blending both consumer behaviour and *Sharia'a* compliance paradigms. The course will also provide a detailed exposition of trade finance, as it is exercised by Islamic banks and the unique practical issues associated with undertaking such activities, including preparation and execution of documentation that complies with both international trade law and *Sharia'a*. Finally, the course will outline the contracts and processes utilised by IFIs to offer banking services such as commitments and guarantees, foreign exchange and payment services.

Islamic Investment Banking

This course will provide a thorough overview of Islamic investment banking as practised today, with a leadership view on potential improvements and innovations in the Islamic investment landscape. Essentially, the course is divided into three major sections: the investment bank operational structure, the deal execution process, and the particular quantitative and qualitative characteristics and methodologies utilised to understand the asset classes conducive to Islamic investment. In doing so, this course also exposes students to the principal modes of investment that IFIs employ because of the asset-backed nature of IFIs, covering all types of equity investment (corporate acquisitions – private equity, real estate, asset-based transactions) and project finance. Each component of the course will also feature the relevant application of *Sharia'a* structuring of financing.

Accounting, Auditing and Governance for Islamic Financial Institutions

This course will provide a comprehensive overview of the governance and accountability dynamics of an Islamic financial institution. The course will expose students to the need for and rationale of the governance mechanisms and rules associated with IFIs (accounting, auditing and *Sharia'a*). In addition, the course will also provide students with a thorough practical grounding of the AAOIFI accounting standards, with a comparative analysis with IFRS standards, where applicable. By the end of the course, students will be able to apply the former standards to analyse the financial statements of IFIs and the extent of compliance with governance norms and rules.

Islamic Treasury, Risk Management and Capital Markets

This course will provide students with an overview of the wholesale operations of IFIs, including inter-bank placements, capital markets operations and products and risk management for IFIs. The course provides a detailed exposition of the specific risks unique to IFIs, and how all risks (including those that are not unique to IFIs) are mitigated/can be mitigated within the parameters of *Sharia'a*. The structuring of a number of unique and innovative risk management products will be discussed, the likes of Islamic profit rate swaps,

Islamic foreign exchange options and Islamic hedging mechanisms. Finally, the course will look into the developments in Islamic capital markets and contemporary issues related to *Sukuk* issuance and trading.

9. Al Huda Centre of Islamic Banking and Economics (Al Huda-CIBE)

The Al Huda Centre of Islamic Banking and Economics (Al Huda-CIBE) was created to provide training in the field of Islamic banking and finance in Punjab and the North West Frontier Province. Al Huda-CIBE has organised more than 90 training sessions/workshops on Islamic banking and finance, *Takaful* and *Sukuk* all over Pakistan. These courses were held mainly at Karachi, Lahore, Islamabad/Rawalpindi, Peshawar, Multan, Faisalabad, Hyderabad, Gujranwala, Mirpur (AJK) and Quetta.

The prime aim of such training and awareness activities is to cultivate an understanding of the spiritual and intellectual heritage of Islam with an emphasis on contributing to the organisation and management of business and finance. Al Huda-CIBE seeks to create a new generation of business leaders, managers, academicians and researchers in this field.

Contact details: www.alhudacibe.com

Al Huda-CIBE is also working with a large number of international institutions as a partner for developing training and awareness in Islamic banking worldwide.

Al Huda-CIBE has created a suite of innovative distance learning courses. These include the following:

1. Postgraduate Diploma in Islamic Banking and Finance (PGD)
2. Certified *Takaful* Professional (CTP)

3. Certified Islamic Fund Manager (CIFM)
4. Certificate in Islamic Microfinance (CIMF).

1. Postgraduate Diploma in Islamic Banking and Finance (PGD)

The Postgraduate Diploma in Islamic Banking and Finance is intended to impart a comprehensive knowledge of Islamic banking and Islamic insurance with its true sense and concepts for participants who are involved or uninvolved with the banking or insurance professions.

The purpose of the PGD is to equip graduates with the *Sharia'a* principles of Islamic finance. This is designed to fulfil the global human resource needs of the industry and produce well-equipped professionals with knowledge of Islamic financial concepts and products.

The aim of the course is to provide educational facilities and training to participants who cannot leave their homes and jobs and also to provide facilities to the masses, providing them with an educational uplift within an Islamic financial system.

The course is designed to serve society by providing affordable and accessible education through the supported technology. Distance learning will be provided to the participants around the globe to disseminate useful knowledge relating to the *Sharia'a*-compliant products, with the participants thereby acquiring appropriate professional skills.

The distance learning course comprises four modules. Each module is of two months' duration. Strong tutorial support is an integral part of the distance learning system. The material provided by the tutorial sessions will help students to update their knowledge according to the latest globally used terms and concepts on Islamic banking *and* finance.

The students will be required to submit their assignments during or at the end of the tutorial sessions. The assignments given to students will be based on the course content.

Al Huda-CIBE has brought together seasoned professionals on its advisory panel to direct and coordinate the Postgraduate Diploma in Islamic Banking and Finance.

Methodology
Communication with the student is made through email. The course contents which consist of CDs, notes, books in PDF format, PowerPoint presentations, literature and reference books and appropriate websites details are sent to the students. The website of Al Huda-CIBE is updated on a daily basis. All the facts, figures, information about admission, programmes and knowledge centre are continuously updated on the website.

The students are provided with email addresses of the advisory panel. They are able to communicate regarding their problems/queries and the advisor will provide timely responses to students' queries.

Module I

Introduction to Islamic Economics

- what is *riba* (interest) – prohibition of *riba* in Islam
- fundamentals of Islamic economics
- distribution of wealth and factors of production in Islam
- IFIs worldwide.

Module II

Islamic Banking

- Islamic financial product mechanisms
- *Musharaka* and *Mudaraba*.
  - basic rules and features of *Musharaka* and *Mudaraba*

- ○ distribution of profit and loss in *Musharaka* and *Mudaraba*.
- diminishing *Musharaka*
  - ○ determine the rental in Diminishing *Musharaka*
  - ○ unit sale mechanism in Diminishing *Musharaka*
  - ○ diminishing *Musharaka* as an ideal product for Islamic housing finance.
- *Bai* (buying and selling)
- basic rules and varieties of *Bai*
- *Bai Murabaha*
- basic features of *Murabaha*
- *Murabaha* as a financing mode
- stages involved in a *Murabaha* sale
- *Sharia'a* compliance and *Murabaha* products
- legal documentation of *Murabaha* contracts
- *Murabaha* in international trade
- practical aspects and issues with *Murabaha*
- case study
- *Bai Salam* and parallel *Salam*
- *Bai Istisna'a*
- difference between *Salam* and *Istisna'a*
- other varieties of *Bai* (*Tawarruq, Bai Musawama, Bai Sarf, Bai Arboun, Bai Inah, Bai Touliya, Bai Wadiah*)
- *Bai* according to quality (*Bai Salah, Bai Fasid, Bai Batil, Sal Maqoof, Bai Majool, Bai Muqayyadah, Bai Mua'ajal*)
- *Ijara* (Islamic lease)
- what is leasing?
- *Sharia'a* alternative – *Ijara*
- *Ijara* (operating lease) versus conventional leasing (financial leasing)
- *Sharia'a* compliance of *Ijara*
- legal framework and documentation for *Ijara* products
- basic feature of *Ijara* contracts and its operational mechanism
- practical aspects and issues with *Ijara*
- *Sukuk* Al *Ijara*
- case study.

Module III

Takaful

- Basic features of *Takaful*
- Structure, operation and performance of *Takaful*
- Different models of *Takaful*
- Legal and regulatory framework with *Takaful*
- *Takaful* products
- Life *Takaful* and general *Takaful*
- Risk management for Islamic banks
- Hedging in Islamic banking
- *Retakaful* and *Bancatakaful*.

Module IV

Islamic Investments, *Sukuk* and Islamic funds

- Islamic investments
- *Sukuk*
- Structuring, operation and performance of *Sukuk*
- Advantages of *Sukuk* issuance and investment
- Worldwide *Sukuk* structures
- Issues and challenges in *Sharia'a*-compliant securitisation
- Creating opportunities in emerging markets
- Issuance of *Sukuk*, factors for consideration
- Case studies
- Islamic funds and Islamic credit cards
- Performance of Islamic funds and investments
- Islamic indices – worldwide.

Duration:	8 months
Number of modules:	4
Duration of one module:	8 weeks
Total number of lessons:	18

For the successful completion of the diploma, students should devote an average of 18 hours in a week for study and submitting the assignments. As the course completion duration is 8 months, students may complete it within 1 year duration.

There is no specific date of admission. Anybody may join the course according to their own convenience. Al Huda-CIBE offers limited seats on a first-come-first-served basis.

FAQs

1. What are the pre-requisites for admission to the PGD course?

- University degree (no experience is required).
- If the student is not a university graduate he must have two years experience.
- There is no age limit.
- English language is the medium of instruction, so its knowledge is a must.
- It is not important to have a background in finance.

2. For whom is this course specially designed?

This course is not for bankers only. Anybody who would like to obtain knowledge of Islamic banking and finance should attend the course. Anybody, whether Muslim or non-Muslim, can be part of the course.

3. What is the admission procedure?

An online application form is available on the website. After receiving the completed form Al Huda-CIBE will send applicants the confirmation. The fee invoices will be sent afterwards. There is no specific date for the start of the course. Participants can start the course at any time.

4. What is the duration of the course?

The total duration of the distance learning Postgraduate Diploma in Islamic Banking and Finance is eight months. The course has four modules and the duration of each module is two months.

5. How can I study for the distance learning diploma course?

Communication with students is made through email. The course contents which will consist of CDs, notes, books, PDF format, PowerPoint presentations, literature and reference books and relevant website details will be sent to the students. The website of Al Huda-CIBE is updated on a daily basis. All the facts, figures, information about admission, programmes and knowledge centre are continuously updated on the website. Students are provided with tutors' email addresses in order that they can communicate with their relevant tutors regarding their problems/queries and tutors will respond to student's queries in a timely manner.

6. In which format will the course material be provided?

When students are enrolled in the diploma course Al Huda-CIBE will send an 'Introductory material set'. This includes the student letter, glossary, enrolment confirmation letter, bibliography and one copy of the Al Huda-CIBE magazine and also the first module lesson. The course material will be in the form of

- notes and presentations in PDF and PPT format
- audio, video lectures
- solved and unsolved case studies
- assignments
- magazines.

7. How will participants receive the course material?

For the first semester, Al Huda-CIBE will send the initial reading material by courier and for the remaining semesters course material will be sent by email.

8. What type of assignments do participants have to solve?

Participants have to solve the questions given at the end of each lesson. In addition, participants will sometimes have to solve some unsolved case studies. Research-based questions will also be given.

9. How will the assignments be submitted?

Participants are instructed to submit each assignment within 2–4 weeks after receiving the module set. Participants may also submit all the assignments at once. Each assignment will be sent by email to the nominated tutor for a specific course.

10. What is the assessment procedure?

After studying the assigned lesson, participants will answer the questions given at the end of the lesson and submit assignments to the tutors and then the tutor will mark the assignments. The tutor will assess the student by their understating of the concepts.

11. What is the tutor satisfaction level?

Participants have to answer the questions from each lesson given to them by their tutor. Participant's answers should match the tutor's requirements and participants should properly cover all the questions asked. Participants will then be able to continue to the next stage of the course.

12. Can participants communicate with the tutor apart from question and answer sessions?

Yes, participants can communicate with the tutor to clarify any subject matter regarding the course through email.

13. What are the pass mark criteria?

Each assignment will carry 100 marks. The pass mark for each assignment is 60%.

14. How will the results be announced?

The tutor will mark the submitted assignments and the mark sheet will be declared with reference to the registration number on the Al Huda website. The result is maintained only by the personal tutor nominated by the Institute. There are no examinations. If participants want to clarify some question or queries, then they should refer these to the course tutor.

15. How will students progress to the next module?

There are no examinations during the course. The tutor's assessment is enough to progress students to the next semester. Each assignment will carry 100 marks. The pass marks in all the assignments will be an aggregate of 60%. No progression will be permitted to participants obtaining less than 60% marks in total assignments. On successful completion of the course participants will be awarded with the PGD certificate.

16. What are the fees?

Fee: US$ 950 (International participants)

There is a subsidised fee for Pakistan, India, Iran and Bangladesh candidates: PKR. 28,000 (fee includes teaching material, reading, audio and video presentations on PPT and PDF format, postal charges, research material and the PGD).

2. Certified Takaful Professional (CTP)

Modules and study details

Duration: 6 months

Number of modules: 2

Duration of each module: 3 months

Module I

Basics of *Takaful*

- Introduction to Islamic economics
- *Riba* (interest) and its varieties
- What is *Takaful*?
- *Sharia'a* mechanisms with *Takaful*
- *Takaful* system in the Islamic era
- Philosophy and development scenario for Islamic insurance
- Comparison of *Takaful* with conventional insurance
- Underlying concepts of Islamic insurance
- Characteristics of mutual insurance.

Sharia'a Elements/Principles in *Takaful*

- Definitions of different *Sharia'a* terms used in *Takaful*
- Concept of *Waqf*
- *Mudaraba*
- Involvement of *Riba*, *Gharar*, *Maisir* and *Qimar* in conventional insurance
- What is *Wakala*?
- *Hibah* and *Tabarru*
- Glossary of *Takaful*.

Module II

Takaful models

- Different models of *Takaful*
- *Wakala–Waqf* model
- *Mudaraba* model
- *Wakala* model
- Surplus distribution mechanism in all models.

Takaful operations and marketing

- Structure, operation and performance of *Takaful*
- Legal and regulatory framework in *Takaful*

- Type of *Takaful*.
  - General *Takaful*
  - Family *Takaful*.
- Micro *Takaful*
- Hedging in Islamic finance
- *Bancatakaful*
- Crop and Livestock *Takaful*
- Methods of marketing family and general *Takaful* products
- *Takaful* products worldwide.

3. Certified Islamic Fund Manager (CIFM)

Modules and study details

Duration: 6 months
Number of modules: 2
Duration of one module: 3 months

Module I

Basics of *Sukuk*

- Introduction to securitisation
- What is Islamic securitisation? A historical perspective
- *Sukuk* – the ever-growing market
- *Sukuk* and securitisation
- The benefits of securitisation
- *Sukuk* characterisation according to AAOIFI
- *Sukuk* viz-a-viz bonds
- *Sukuk* and conventional bonds: a comparison.

Introduction to Islamic Finance

- What is *riba* (interest) – prohibition of *riba* in Islam
- Fundamentals of Islamic economics.

Islamic Financial Products

- ### *Musharaka* and *Mudaraba*
  - The basic rules and features of *Musharaka* and *Mudaraba*
  - Distribution of profit and loss in *Musharaka* and *Mudaraba*.
- ### Diminishing *Musharaka*
  - Determining the rental in Diminishing *Musharaka*
  - Unit sale mechanism in Diminishing *Musharaka*
  - Diminishing *Musharaka* as an ideal product for Islamic housing finance.
- ### Sale-based modes of Islamic finance – *Bai* (buying and selling)
  - Basic rules and varieties of *Bai*
  - *Bai Murabaha*
    - Basic features of *Murabaha*
    - *Murabaha* as a financing mode
    - Stages involved in the *Murabaha* sale
    - *Sharia'a* compliance and *Murabaha* products
    - Legal documentation of *Murabaha* contracts
    - *Murabaha* in international trade
    - Practical aspects and issues with *Murabaha*
    - Case study
    - *Bai Salam* and parallel *Salam*
    - *Bai Istisna'a*.
  - Difference between *Salam* and *Istisna'a*
  - Other varieties of *Bai* (*Tawarruq, Bai Musawama, Bai Sarf, Bai Arboun, Bai Inah, Bai Touliya, Bai Wadiah*)
  - *Bai* according to quality (*Bai Salah, Bai Fasid, Bai Batil, Bai Magoof, Bai Majool, Bai Muqayyadah, Bai Mua'ajal*).
- ### *Ijara* (Islamic lease)
  - What is leasing?
  - *Sharia'a* alternative – *Ijara*
  - *Ijara* (operating lease) versus conventional leasing
  - *Sharia'a* compliance of *Ijara*
  - Legal framework and documentations for *Ijara* products
  - Basic feature of *Ijara* contracts and its operational mechanism

- ○ Practical aspects and issues with *Ijara*
- ○ *Sukuk Al Ijara*
- ○ Case study.

Module II

- *Sharia'a* **principles of** *Sukuk*
  - ○ AAOIFI *Sharia'a* standards for issuing *Sukuk*
  - ○ Various types of investment *Sukuk* under AAOIFI standards
  - ○ Issues and challenges in order to make *Sukuk Sharia'a* compliant
  - ○ Some regulatory aspects of *Sukuk*.
- Issuance process
  - ○ Parties involved
  - ○ Flow
  - ○ Distribution methods
  - ○ Documentation
  - ○ Structuring considerations
  - ○ Advantages of issuing *Sukuk*
  - ○ Advantages of *Sukuk* investing
  - ○ Parties involved in issuing *Sukuk*
  - ○ Market challenges
  - ○ Credit rating of *Sukuk*
  - ○ *Takaful* and hedging with *Sukuk*.
- **AAOIFI** *Sukuk* **structure**
  - ○ *Salam* certificates
  - ○ *Istisna'a* certificates
  - ○ *Murabaha* certificates
  - ○ *Musharaka* certificates
  - ○ *Muzara'a* (sharecropping) certificates
  - ○ *Musaqah* certificates
  - ○ *Mugharasaha* certificates
  - ○ Certificates of ownership in leased assets
  - ○ Certificates of ownership of usufructs
  - ○ Certificates of ownership of usufructs of existing assets
  - ○ Certificates of ownership of usufructs of described future assets

- ○ Certificates of ownership of services of a specific party
- ○ Certificates of ownership of described future services.
- **Structuring and operation of *Sukuk***
  - ○ Creating opportunities in emerging markets
  - ○ Structuring, operation and performance of *Sukuk*
  - ○ Issues and challenges in *Sharia'a*-compliant securitisation
  - ○ The phases in structuring *Sukuk*
  - ○ *Sharia'a* issues
  - ○ Secondary market for *Sukuk*
  - ○ Trading of debt securities
  - ○ *Bay' al Dayn* with discounting
  - ○ Legal documentation and related issues
  - ○ Cross-border listing of *Sukuk*
  - ○ Legal requirements for issuing *Sukuk*.
- **Other aspects to be considered**
  - ○ Issuing *Sukuk*
  - ○ Cost efficiency
  - ○ Taxation issues
  - ○ Cheaper cost of funds
  - ○ Credit rating
  - ○ Investing in *Sukuk*
  - ○ Return on investment
  - ○ Risk and return profile
  - ○ Liquidity and tradability of the *Sukuk*.

Certificate in Islamic Microfinance (CIMF)

Islamic microfinance is a new emerging discipline in the field of Islamic finance. There is an immediate need to have a comprehensive education, training, market study and awareness on this subject. Al Huda-CIBE offers a specialised comprehensive certificate programme on Islamic microfinance on a distance learning basis. It is a highly structured, interactive and innovatively designed programme under the supervision of a panel of academicians, *Sharia'a* scholars and professionals.

The aim of the course is to provide educational facilities and training to participants who cannot leave their homes and jobs with an additional opportunity for their educational uplift under the Islamic financial system. The Certified Islamic Microfinance programme comprises two modules, each of two months duration. Strong tutorial support is an integral part of the distance learning system. The material provided by the tutorial sessions will help students to update their knowledge according to the latest terms and concepts globally used in Islamic microfinance.

Modules and study details

Duration:	4 months
Number of modules:	2
Duration of one module:	2 months

Module I
***Sharia'a* foundation and applications in micro/rural finance**

- conceptual framework of Islamic micro/rural finance
- *Riba* and the prohibition of *riba*
- economic rationale for the prohibition of *riba*
- the basic framework of the Islamic financial system
- compatibility of microfinance with the Islamic modes of finance.

Sale-based modes in Islamic microfinance

- *Murabaha*
  - Basic features of *Murabaha*
  - *Murabaha* as financing mode in the micro/rural finance sector
  - Steps involved in a *Murabaha* sale
  - *Sharia'a* compliance and *Murabaha* products
  - Practical aspects and Issues with *Murabaha*.

- *Salam*
  - Basic features of *Salam*
  - *Salam* as financing mode in the micro/rural finance sector
  - Steps involved in a *Salam* sale
  - Parallel *Salam*.
- *Istisna'a*
  - What is *Istisna'a*?
  - *Istisna'a* as a financing mode in the micro/rural finance sector
  - Procedure involved in *Salam* sale
  - Difference between *Istisna'a* and *Salam*
  - Difference between *Istisna'a* and *Ijara*.
- **An overview of conventional microfinance**
  - Microfinance – considered as a tool for poverty alleviation
  - Microfinance – characteristics
  - Outreach and sustainability problems
  - Microfinance programme's sustainability.

Module II
Profit and loss – sharing instruments of micro/rural finance

- *Mudaraba*
  - The basic rules and features of *Mudaraba*
  - Types of *Mudaraba*
  - Restricted *Mudaraba*
  - Unrestricted *Mudaraba*
  - Profit and loss distribution in *Mudaraba*
  - Termination of a *Mudaraba*.
- *Musharaka*
  - The basic rules and features of *Musharaka*
  - Type of *Musharaka*
  - *Shirkat–ul-Milk*
  - *Shirkat-ul-Aqd*
  - Profit and loss distribution in *Musharaka*
  - Management of *Musharaka*
  - Termination of *Musharaka*
  - The difference between *Musharaka* and *Mudaraba*.

Rental-based mechanisms in Islamic micro/rural finance

- *Ijara* (Islamic lease)
  - What is *Ijara*?
  - *Sharia'a* principles of *Ijara* (operating lease)) versus conventional leasing (financial leasing)
  - *Sharia'a* compliance of *Ijara*.
- Diminishing *Musharaka*
  - Determining the rental in diminishing *Musharaka*
  - Unit sale mechanism in diminishing *Musharaka*
  - Diminishing *Musharaka* as an ideal product for micro housing finance.
- Liability (deposit) management techniques for Islamic microfinance
- Product development for Islamic microfinance.

Appendix: Testing Locations

All CBT-enabled examinations are available at Thomson Prometric professional testing centres in all of the following cities and countries:

Canada and Central/South America	United States of America	UK, IOM and Channel Islands	Europe	Africa	India	China	Asia/Australasia/Middle East
Canada–Calgary, Edmonton, Ottawa, Toronto	Albany, NY	Basildon	Denmark–Copenhagen	Botswana–Gaborone	Bangalore	Beijing	Australia–Melbourne, Sydney
	Boston, MA	Belfast	Eire–Dublin	Egypt–Cairo	Calcutta	Chagsha	Hong Kong
	Brooklyn Heights, NY	Birmingham	France–Paris	Ghana–Accra	Chennai	Chengdu	Japan–Tokyo
	Buffalo, NY	Bournemouth	Germany–Frankfurt, Munich	Kenya–Nairobi	Gurgaon	Dalian	Kuwait–Kuwait City
	Chicago, IL	Bristol	Greece–Athens	Mauritius–Port Louis	Hyderabad	Guangzhou	Lebanon–Beirut
	Cincinnati, OH	Cardiff	Hungary–Budapest	Nigeria–Lagos	Mumbai	Harbin	Malaysia–Kuala Lumpur
	Columbus, OH	Edinburgh	Italy–Milan	South Africa–Cape Town, Johannesburg		Jinan	New Zealand–Auckland
	Coral Springs, FL	Glasgow	Portugal–Lisbon	Tanzania–Dar Es Salaam		Kunming	Saudi Arabia–Riyadh–Men, Riyadh–Women
	Melville, NY	Guernsey	Russia–Moscow	Uganda–Kampala		Nanjing	Singapore
	Miami, FL	Isle of Man	Spain–Barcelona, Madrid	Zimbabwe–Harare		Shanghai	UAE–Dubai
	New York City, NY	Jersey	Switzerland–Geneva			Wuhan	
	Rochester, NY	Leeds				Xi'an	
	San Francisco, CA	Liverpool				Xiamen	
	Syracuse, NY	London–Pellipar House					
	Westbury, NY	London–SII site					
		Manchester					
		Newcastle					
		Peterborough					
		Southampton					

Chapter 7

How Much Arabic do you Need to Know to Work in the Industry?

*Y*ou certainly do not need to be able to speak fluent Arabic. However, there is a certain minimum number of terms you do need to know. These do not translate easily, so the Arabic terminology is always used. The spelling of the terms also varies widely. The key terms are presented below, arranged alphabetically.

Amanah

In *Sharia'a*, the concept of justice and faithfulness is called *Amanah*. The term *Amanah* means that reward and punishment are linked, Muslims believe, with the fulfilment of obligations incurred under the stipulations of a contract. Justice links man to Allah and to his fellow men, Muslims believe. It is this bond that forms the contractual foundation of the *Sharia'a*, which judges the virtue of justice in man not only by his material performance but also by the essential attribute of the intention with which a man enters into every contract. This intention consists of sincerity, truthfulness, and insistence on rigorous and loyal fulfilment of what he has consented to do (or not to do).

This faithfulness to one's contractual obligations is so central to Islamic believers that when the Prophet Mohammed was asked 'who is the believer?' He replied that 'a believer is a person in whom the people can trust their person and possessions'. He is also reported to have said that 'a person without trustworthiness is a person without religion'. So basic is the notion of contracts in Islam that every public office is regarded, primarily, as a contract and an agreement which defines the rights and obligations of the parties.

Amanah, at a more general level, is associated with trustworthiness, faithfulness and honesty.

As an important secondary meaning, *Amanah* also identifies a transaction where one party keeps another's funds or property in trust. This is in fact the most widely understood and used application of the term, and has a long history of use in Islamic commercial law. By extension, the term can also be used to describe different financial or commercial activities such as deposit taking, custody or holding goods on consignment.

This holding of deposits in trust has important legal implications. A person can hold a property in trust for another, sometimes by express contract and sometimes by implication of a contract. *Amanah*, in this context, entails an absence of liability for loss except in the breach of duty. Current accounts are regarded as *Amanah* (trust) accounts. If a bank is given authority to use current account funds in its business, *Amanah* transforms into a loan. Banks are legally obliged to repay the full amount of current accounts.

The antonym of *Amanah* is *khayan*, meaning betrayal, faithlessness and treachery.

Arboun

This is a sale agreement in which a security deposit, known as *Hamish gedyyah*, is provided in advance as part payment towards the price of the commodity. The deposit is forfeited if the buyer does not meet his obligations.

So *Arboun* is an amount of money paid by the purchase orderer upon the request of the seller to ensure that he is serious in his order of the asset/shares. If the promise is binding and the purchase orderer declines to purchase the asset, the actual loss incurred to the seller is made good from this deposit.

Hamish gedyyah is a security deposit and is a term sometimes associated with *Arboun* but also with *Murabaha* and other *Sharia'a* nominate contracts.

'Aariyah

'Aariyah refers to the gratuitous loan of non-fungible objects. More precisely, 'Aariyah means the loan of a particular piece of property, the substance of which is not consumed by being used, without anything taken in exchange. In other words, it is the gift of usufruct of a property or commodity that is not consumed when used. It is different from Qard (c.f.) which involves the loan of fungible objects which are consumed when used and in which a similar and not the same commodity has to be returned. 'Aariyah is also deemed to be a virtuous act, like Qard. The borrowed commodity is treated as liability of the borrower who is bound to return it to its owner.

So 'Aariyah is a contract in which one party loans another the use of some item for an indefinite period of time. 'Aariyah is generally used to refer to the neighbourly lending of small articles.

Bai'

Bai' means sale, an agreement between two parties (the seller and the buyer) to the effect that the ownership of the sale item is transferred from the seller to the buyer in exchange for a price or payment.

Bai' Bithaman Ajil (BBA)

This contract refers to the sale of goods on a deferred payment basis. Equipment or goods requested by a client are bought by the bank which subsequently sells the goods to the client at an agreed price which includes the bank's mark-up (profit). The client may be allowed to settle payment by instalments within a pre-agreed period, or in a lump sum. This is similar to a Murabaha contract, as it is a credit sale, but with payment on a deferred basis.

Bai' Muajjal

Literally, this means a credit sale. Technically, it is a financing technique adopted by Islamic banks that takes the form of *Murabaha Muajjal*. It is a contract in which the seller earns a profit margin on his purchase price and allows the buyer to pay the price of the commodity at a future date in a lump sum or in instalments. The seller has to expressly mention the cost of the commodity, and the margin of profit is mutually agreed upon. It is also applied between a wholesaler and a retailer for the supply of a number of agreed items.

Bai' Istijrar

Under this contract, a supplier agrees to deliver to a client, on a regular basis, at an agreed price and mode of payment. *Istijrar* literally means a recurring sale. It is a term used where different quantities are bought from a single seller over a period of time. Sometimes it also refers to transactions whereby the seller delivers different quantities in different instalments to complete the full purchase.

Bai' bil Wafa

This is a sale with a right to the seller that enables him to repurchase (redeem) the property by refunding the purchase price. It is a *Bai'* in form but a pledge in substance. So it is a sale with the right of redemption, literally, a sale of honour. According to the majority of *Fuqaha*, this is not a *Sharia' a*-compliant contract.

Bai' Muzayadah

This is an action by a person selling an asset in the open market, which is accompanied by the process of bidding amongst potential buyers. The asset for sale will be given to the person who offered the highest price in open bidding.

In other words, it is a sale and purchase transaction based on an auction/tender.

Batil

Literally, this means void or invalid. It refers to a contract which governs a transaction, or an element in such a contract, which makes it null and void.

Daman

This is a contract of guarantee whereby a guarantor will underwrite any claim and obligation that should be fulfilled by the owner of the asset. This concept is also applicable to a guarantee provided on a debt transaction in the event a debtor fails to fulfil his debt obligation.

Darura

Darura means necessity. In an emergency, Muslims may disregard aspects of *Sharia'a* law in order to save their lives or to preserve the Islamic community, for example, drinking alcohol or eating pork if it will save your life.

Dayn

Dayn means debt, that is, some form of debt which one is required to pay back to another. A *Dayn* comes into existence as a result of a contract or a credit transaction. It is incurred either by way of rent or sale or purchase or in any other way which results in a debt to another. *Duyun* (debts) should be returned without any profit since they are advanced to help the needy and to meet their demands. The lender should not impose on the borrower more than what he has given on credit.

Bai' al-Dayn

Bai' al-Dayn means the sale of debt or receivables. This would be a transaction that involves the sale and purchase of securities or debt certificates that conform with the *Sharia'a*. Securities or debt certificates are issued by a debtor to a creditor as evidence of indebtedness.

Bai' al-Dayn involves the provision of financial resources required for manufacturing, commerce and services through the sale and purchase of trade documents and commercial paper. *Bai' al-Dayn* is a short-term facility with a year or less of maturity. Only documents that evidence debts arising from bona fide commercial transactions can be traded.

Bai' al-kali' bil-kali'

Literally, this means the sale of a debt for a debt. *Bay' al-kali' bil-kali'* is a type of sale which is prohibited under the *Sharia'a*. Islamic jurists use this term to describe several different types of debt-for-debt exchanges. The most well known of these is the exchange in which a lender extends his debtor's debt repayment period in return for an increase on the principal, that is, interest.

The term *kali'* is a synonym for debt. *Kali'* refers to something delayed and appears in a maxim (*Hadith*) forbidding the sale of *al-kali' bil-kali'*, that is, the exchange of one delayed counter value for another delayed counter value.

Counter value

A counter value means an equivalent value. Counter values are the price and the subject matter in a *Sharia'a* contract. *Sharia'a* law requires that either the price is paid or the subject matter is delivered, at the time of the contract. To validate a sale, from the perspective of the *Sharia'a*, it is necessary that at least one, if not both, of the counter values should be present at the time of the contract. Either the price or the delivery of the subject matter may be postponed to a future date, but not both.

Fasid

This refers to an action which is unsound or unviable. It refers to a forbidden term in a contract, which consequently renders the contract invalid.

Fatwa and Fatawa (Pl)

A *fatwa* is an Islamic religious ruling, a scholarly opinion on a matter of Islamic law.

A *fatwa* is issued by a recognised religious authority in Islam. But since there is no hierarchical priesthood or anything of that sort in Islam, a *fatwa* is not necessarily 'binding' on the faithful. The persons who pronounce these rulings are supposed to be knowledgeable, and base their rulings on this knowledge and wisdom. They need to supply the contextual evidence from Islamic sources for their opinions, and it is not uncommon for scholars to come to different conclusions regarding the same issue.

According to the *Sharia'a* principles of jurisprudence, a *fatwa* must meet the following conditions in order to be valid:

1. The *fatwa* must be in line with relevant legal proofs, deduced from Qur'anic verses and *ahadith*, provided the *ahadith* was not later abrogated by the Prophet Mohammed.
2. It must be issued by a person (or a *Sharia'a* board) having due knowledge and sincerity of heart.
3. It must be free from individual opportunism, and not depend on political servitude.
4. It must meet the needs of the contemporary world.

The plural of *fatwa* is *fatawa*.

Fiqh, Faqih and Fuqaha (Pl)

Fiqh is Islamic law, sometimes incorrectly called *Sharia'a law*. It refers to the practical jurisprudence or human articulations of divine rules encompassing both law and ethics. *Fiqh* may be understood as the Islamic jurists' interpretation of the *Sharia'a*, or jurists' law.

A *Faqih* is a Muslim jurist, a Muslim who is an expert in *Fiqh*. This would be a Muslim who is knowledgeable of the rules of the *Sharia'a* and knows how these rules are related to the source texts upon which they are based.

The plural of *Faqih* is *Fuqaha*.

Fiqh al-Mu'amalat

Literally, this means an economic transaction. Technically, it refers to the lease of land or of fruit trees for money, or for a share of the crop. *Fiqh al-Mu'amalat* is Islamic commercial jurisprudence, the rules for transacting in a *Sharia'a*-compliant manner.

It is an important source for establishing the rules for Islamic banking.

Husah (gharar)

Literally, this means pebbles. It was a type of sale practised by the Arabs in the *Jahiliyyah* (pre-Islamic times) in which the sale was determined by the casting of pebbles. It was prohibited by the Prophet Mohammed. Classical commentators mention three forms of the *husah* sale:

1. The seller would say to the would-be purchaser, 'when I throw the pebbles in my hand, then the deal is closed and binding on you'.

2. The seller would say to the would-be purchaser, 'I shall sell you the commodity which your pebbles hit'.
3. In a land sale, the seller would say, 'I shall sell you the plot of land whose dimensions are defined by the extent to which you throw this pebble'.

The *husah* sale was ostensibly prohibited because of the *gharar* (uncertainty) which characterised the contract which governed it.

Gharar

This refers to uncertainty, hazard, chance or risk in a contractual arrangement. It is one of the three fundamental prohibitions in Islamic finance (the other two being *riba* and *maisir*).

Gharar is an element of deception either through ignorance of the goods, the price, or through faulty description of the goods, in which one or both parties stand to be deceived through ignorance of an essential element of the exchange. Gambling is a form of *gharar* because the gambler is ignorant of the result of the gamble.

Gharar is a sophisticated concept that covers certain types of uncertainty or contingency in a contract. The prohibition associated with *gharar* is often used as the grounds for criticism of conventional financial practices such as short selling, speculation and derivatives.

Gharar is divided into three types, namely, *gharar fahish* (excessive), which vitiates the transaction, *gharar yasir* (minor), which is tolerated, and *gharar mutawassit* (moderate), which falls between the other two categories. Any transaction can be classified as an Islamically forbidden activity because of excessive *gharar*.

Technically, *gharar* means the sale of a thing which is not present at hand; or the sale of a thing whose consequence or outcome is not known; or a sale involving risk of hazard in which one does not know whether it will come to be or not, such as selling fish in the sea or a bird in the air. It includes deception through ignorance by one or more parties to a contract.

There are several varieties of *gharar*, all of which are *haram*. The following are some examples:

- selling goods that the seller is unable to deliver;
- selling known or unknown goods against an unknown price;
- selling goods without giving a proper description;
- selling goods without specifying the price;
- making a contract conditional on an unknown event;
- selling goods on the basis of a false description;
- selling goods without allowing the buyer to examine them properly.

Al Ghunm bil Ghurm

Literally, this means 'no reward without taking risks.' This principle provides the rationale for profit sharing in *Shirkah* arrangements. Earning profit is legitimised only by engaging in an economic venture involving risk-sharing which ultimately contributes to economic development. See also *Kharaj bi-al-Daman*.

Halal

This refers to anything permitted by the *Sharia'a* – in effect a deed which is not prohibited by Allah.

The concept of *halal* has spiritual and religious overtones. In Islam there are activities, professions, contracts and transactions that are explicitly prohibited (*haram*) by the *Qur'an*. All other activities, professions, contracts and transactions are *halal*.

This concept differentiates Islamic economics from conventional economics. In western finance all activities are judged on economic utility. In Islamic economics, spiritual and moral factors are also involved. An activity may be economically sound but may not be allowed in Islamic society.

Haram

This is anything prohibited by the *Sharia'a*. In effect, it is a deed which is prohibited by Allah.

Hawala

Legally, this is a bill of exchange, promissory note, cheque or draft. More technically, a debtor passes on the responsibility of payment of his debt to a third party who owes the former a debt. Thus the responsibility of payment is ultimately shifted to a third party. *Hawala* is a mechanism which can be usefully employed for settling international accounts by book transfer. This obviates, to a large extent, the necessity of physical transfer of cash.

The term was also used, historically, during the *Abbasid* period (AD 750–1258), to refer to cases where the State Treasury could not meet the claims presented to it and it directed its claimants to occupy a certain region for a certain period and procure their claims themselves by taxing the people. This method was also known as *tasabbub*. The taxes collected and transmitted to the central treasury were known as *mahmul* (i.e. carried to the treasury) while those assigned to the claimants or provinces were known as *musabbab*.

Hibah

This means gift or donation. Technically, this means a transfer of a defined property (*mal*) without any material consideration. Muslims have been exhorted by the Prophet to donate gifts to others. This is one of the important values of a Muslim society. It is intended to cultivate love and cooperation among citizens, rather than rivalry and competition.

Ibra'

This is an act by a person to withdraw his rights, that is, his rights to collect payment from a person who has the obligation to repay the amount borrowed from him. It usually refers to a kind of rebate. The creditor gives up part or all of his contractual rights to a debtor usually for early settlement of a debt.

Ijara

Ijara is a form of leasing in which there is a transfer of ownership of a service for a specified period for an agreed lawful consideration. Instead of lending money and earning interest, *Ijara* allows the financial institution to earn profits by charging rent on the asset leased to the customer.

So *Ijara* is leasing, the sale of a definite usufruct (c.f.) of any asset in exchange for definite reward. It refers to a contract of land leased at a fixed rent payable in cash and also to a mode of financing adopted by Islamic banks. *Ijara* is an arrangement under which an Islamic bank leases equipment, buildings or other facilities to a client, against an agreed rental.

In practice, there is a lease agreement whereby a bank or financier buys an item for a customer and then leases it to him over a specific period, thus earning profits for the bank by charging rent.

The duration of the lease and the fee are set in advance. During the period of the lease, the asset remains in the ownership of the lessor (the bank) but the lessee has the right to use it. After the expiry of the lease agreement, this right reverts back to the lessor.

Leasing is a lawful method of earning income, according to *Sharia'a* law. In practice, real assets such as a machine, a car, a ship or a house can be leased by one person (lessor) to the other (lessee) for a specific period against a specific price. The benefit and cost of each party are to be clearly spelled out in the contract so as to ensure that any ambiguity (*gharar*) is avoided.

Ijara Muntahia Bittamleek (Ijara-wa-Iqtina)

These are *Ijara* contracts that end up with the transfer of ownership of leased assets to the lessee. *Ijara Muntahia Bittamleek* may take one of the following forms:

1. *Ijara Muntahia Bittamleek* that transfers the ownership of leased assets to the lessee, if the lessee so desires, for a price represented by the rental payments made by the lessee over the lease term. At the end of the lease term, and after the last instalment is paid, legal title of leased assets passes automatically to the lessee on the basis of a new contract.
2. *Ijara Muntahia Bittamleek* that gives the lessee the right of ownership of leased assets at the end of the lease term on the basis of a new contract, for a specified price. This may be for a token price.
3. *Ijara* agreement that gives the lessee one of three options that the lessee may exercise at the end of the lease term:
   - purchasing the leased asset for a price that is determined based on rental payments made by the lessee;
   - renewal of *Ijara* for another term; or
   - returning the leased asset to the lessor (owner).

So it is a lease and purchase transaction. It is a financing instrument used in contemporary Islamic finance in which a financier purchases reusable merchandise (e.g. airplane, buildings, cars) and then leases them to clients in return for an agreed upon rental fee (to be paid for the length of the lease period) and an agreement that the client will purchase the merchandise at the end of the lease period.

This technique is sometimes called *Ijara Thumma Bai.*

Ijtihad

Literally this means effort, exertion or diligence. *Ijtihad* refers to the endeavours of a qualified jurist to derive or formulate a rule of law to determine the true ruling of the divine law in a matter on which the revelation is not explicit or certain. This would be on the basis of *Nass*, or evidence, found in the *Qur'an* and the *Sunnah.*

So *Ijtihad* refers to the process by which a qualified Islamic jurist (called a *Mujtahid*) endeavours to arrive at the correct *Sharia'a* ruling on a given issue by reflecting on source texts from the fundamental sources of the *Sharia'a*: the *Qur'an* and *Sunnah.*

Ijma'

Literally, this means consensus. In this context, it would be the unanimous consensus of the Muslim *Ummah* on a given issue, usually as represented by the agreement of the jurists. *Ijma'* has traditionally been recognised as an independent source of *Sharia'a* law, along with the *Qur'an*, *Sunnah* and *Qiyas* (analogical deduction), by most of the jurists.

'Inah

This is a loan in the form of a sale. It is called *'inah* (meaning façade) because it is a sale in appearance only. This is accomplished by the customer buying back what the customer has sold for a lower price than that for which the customer originally sold it. The difference, ostensibly profit, is actually a loan.

Bai al-'inah is a double sale by which the borrower and the lender sell and then resell an object between them, once for cash and once for a higher price on credit, with the net result being a loan with interest. This is deemed to be non-*Sharia'a* compliant by GCC scholars, but is acceptable in Malaysia.

It can also be applied vice versa where a financier buys an asset from a customer on cash terms. Immediately afterwards, the financier sells back the same asset to the customer on deferred payment terms at a price higher than that of the cash sale.

'Inan

This is a form of financial partnership in which each partner contributes capital and has the right to work for the business, not necessarily on an equal basis with the other partners.

Islam

Literally, this means submission to Allah. It refers to the religion of Allah (God), that is, the worship of Allah alone.

A person whose religion is Islam is a Muslim. A person becomes a Muslim by declaring the *Shahada*, that is, 'Ashhadu an la ilaha illallah wa ashhadu anna Muhammadan rasulullah' ('I testify that there is nothing rightfully worshipped except Allah and I testify that Muhammad is the Messenger of Allah').

Islam is based on five pillars. These are as follows:

1. *Shahada*, that is, testifying that there is no god but Allah and that Mohammed is the Messenger of Allah;
2. Undertaking *Salah*, that is, prescribed prayer;
3. Paying *zakat*, that is, giving a portion of one's wealth to the needy;
4. The *Sawm of Ramadan*, that is, fasting during the ninth month of the Islamic calendar;
5. *Hajj*, that is, making pilgrimage to the sacred precincts of Mecca, in Saudi Arabia, once in a lifetime, if one is able and can afford it.

Istihsan

This is a doctrine of *Sharia'a* law that allows exceptions to strict legal reasoning, involving guiding choice among possible legal outcomes. It is usually applied when considerations of human welfare so demand.

Istisna'a

Istisna'a is a contractual agreement for manufacturing goods and commodities, allowing cash payment in advance and future delivery or a future payment and future delivery. A manufacturer or builder agrees to produce or build a clearly described good or building at a given price on a given date in the future. The price can be paid in instalments, step by step as agreed between the parties. *Istisna'a* can be used for financing the manufacture or construction of houses, plant, building of bridges, roads, power stations and so on.

Parallel Istisna'a

If *al-mustasni'a* (the ultimate purchaser) in an *Istisna'a* contract does not stipulate in the contract that *al-sani'* (the seller) should manufacture the *al-masnoo'* (the product) by himself, then *al-sani'* may enter into a second *Istisna'a* contract in order to fulfil his contractual obligations in the first contract. The second contract is called a *Parallel Istisna'a*.

Jahala

This refers to ignorance, lack of knowledge or indefiniteness in a contract, sometimes leading to *gharar*.

Jua'alah or Ji'alah

Literally, *Jua'alah* constitutes wages, pay, stipend or reward. Legally, it is a contract for performing a given task against a prescribed fee in a given period. A similar contract is *Ujrah* in which any work is done against a stipulated wage or fee. *Jua'alah* is a contract of reward. It is a unilateral contract promising a reward for a specific act or accomplishment.

Bank charges and commission have been interpreted to be a *Jua'alah* by the jurists and thus considered lawful.

Some Islamic banks give loans which involve service charges. The Council of the Islamic Fiqh Academy established by the Organisation of Islamic Conference, in its third session held in October 1986, in response to a query from the Islamic Development Bank has resolved that it is permitted to charge a fee for loan-related service offered by an Islamic bank.

However, this fee should be related to actual expenditures and any fee in excess of this is forbidden because it is considered usurious. The service charge may be calculated accurately only after a certain period when all administrative expenditure has already been incurred, for example, at the end of the year. Hence, it is permissible to levy an approximate charge to the client, then, reimburse or claim the difference at the end of the accounting period when the actual expenses on administration become precisely known.

Kafalah (Suretyship)

Literally, *Kafalah* means responsibility, or suretyship. Legally, in *Kafalah*, a third party becomes a surety for the payment of a debt. It is a pledge given to a creditor that the debtor will pay the debt, fine and so on. Suretyship in Islamic law is the creation of an additional liability with regard to the claim, not to the debt itself.

So *Kafalah* is the assumption of the responsibility for debt repayment. It is a standard Islamic financial transaction in which X (the *kafil*) agrees to assume responsibility for the debts of Y (the *makful 'anhu*). It is similar but not identical to *hawala*.

Kharaj bi-al-Daman

Literally, this means 'with profit comes responsibility.' Sometimes, it is translated as 'gain accompanies liability for loss.' It is a *Hadith* forming a legal maxim and a basic principle in Islamic finance. See *Al Ghunm bil Ghurm*.

Khiyar

Literally, this means option or choice. It is the option extended, to one or more of the parties in a sales contract, to rescind the sale in the event of a defect.

The jurists have traditionally recognised several different types of *khiyar*, including *khiyar al-majlis*, *khiyar al-shart*, *khiyar al-ru'yah* and *khiyar al-'ayb*. *Khiyar*, more explicitly referring to trading contracts, comes in several varieties:

> *Khiyar al-majlis*: Option of the contracting session; the power to annul a contract possessed by both contracting parties as long as they do not separate.

> *Khiyar al-shart*: An option in a sale contract concluded at the time of signing the agreement, giving one of the two

parties to the contract a right to cancel the sale within a stipulated time.

Madhab, Madhabib (Pl)

Literally, this means a way of going. It refers to a *Fiqh* school of law or orientation characterised by differences in the methods by which certain Islamic source texts are interpreted, and therefore differences in the *Sharia'a* rulings which are deduced from them.

There are four well-known *Madhahib*, among *Sunni* Muslims, whose names are associated with the classical jurists who are said to have founded them (*Hanafi*, *Maliki*, *Shafi'i* and *Hanbali*). These are as follows:

Hanbali: Founded by Imam Ahmad Ibn Hanbal. Followers of this school are known as *Hanbali's*.

Hanafi: Founded by Imam Abu Hanifa. Followers of this school are known as *Hanafi's*.

Maliki: Founded by Imam Malik Ibn Anas. Followers of this school are known as *Malikis*.

Shafi'i: Founded by Abu Abdullah Ahmad bin Idris or Imam Shafii. Followers of this school are known as *Shafi'is*.

Maisir

Maisir is gambling – any activity that involves betting money, or an item, on the outcome of an unpredictable event. The bet is forfeited if the outcome is not as predicted by the bettor and the person against whom the bet is made takes the stake. This activity is prohibited by the *Sharia'a*.

Gambling is a game of chance. Originally it refers to a game of chance played by the Arabs before Islam. *Maisir* refers to any game of chance. It is one of the three fundamental prohibitions in Islamic finance (the other two being *riba* and *gharar*).

The prohibition on *maisir* is often used as the grounds for the non-permissibility of conventional financial practices such as speculation, conventional insurance and derivatives.

Makruh

Literally this means detested. It is a technical term used by the *Fuqaha* (c.f.) to classify actions with regard to their desir-ability. The term *makruh* refers to an action in which one is rewarded Islamically for avoiding certain actions, but not punished for committing them.

Mal

The word money is not specifically mentioned in the *Qu'ran*. The nearest word mentioned in the *Qu'ran* is *mal* meaning wealth, money, property – any valuable thing which can be possessed. The term is used in the sense of something that has value and can be gainfully used according to the *Sharia'a*.

The term *mal* is used in a variety of contexts:

Rab-al-mal: In a *Mudaraba* contract the person who invests the capital.

Ra's al-mal: Capital. This refers to the money or property which an investor (*rab-al-mal*) invests in a profit-seeking venture, often in a partnership such as *Mudaraba* or *Musharaka* arrangement.

Bayt al-mal: Historically, this refers to the Treasury of the Muslim community. The *bayt al-mal*, as an institution, was developed by the early Caliphs but it soon fell into disre-pair. The funds contained in the *bayt al-mal* were meant to be spent on the needs of the *Umma*, for example, support-ing the needy.

Manfa'a

Literally, this term means benefit. It is usually used in the context of *Ijara*. It is used to refer to the yield which utilisable property produces.

The term is often used by the *Fuqaha* to describe the usufruct (c.f.) associated with a given property, especially in leasing transactions. In a car lease, for example, the term *Manfa'a* might be used to describe the benefit which the lessee derives from the use of the car for the duration of the lease (as opposed to the actual ownership of the vehicle).

Maqasid al-Sharia'a

This term generally refers to the objectives of *Sharia'a* law. The term *Maqasid al-Sharia'a* refers to a juristic philosophical concept developed by the later generations of classical jurists, who attempted to formulate the goals and purposes of the *Sharia'a* in a comprehensive manner to aid in the process of investigating new cases and organising earlier existing rulings.

Mithli (fungible goods)

Mithli are fungible goods, that is, goods that can be returned in kind, for example, gold for gold, silver for silver, $US for $US, wheat for wheat and so on.

Mudarib

The managing partner in a *Mudaraba* contract.

Mudaraba (Trust Financing)

This is an agreement made between two parties, one of whom provides 100% of the capital for the project and who has no control over the management of the project and another party known as a *Mudarib*, who manages the project using his entrepreneurial skills. Profits arising from the project are distributed according to a predetermined ratio. Losses are borne by the provider of capital.

Mugharasaha (munasabah)

This refers to a type of agricultural contract in which a land owner and a worker agree that, in return for the worker's planting and tending of fruit-bearing trees on the land owner's field, the landowner will assign to the worker a share of the orchard's harvest. Both *Hanafi* and *Hanbali* jurists (the latter also called the transaction *munasabah*) discuss *Mugharasaha* in their *Fiqh* works.

Two valid forms of the contract exist:

1. The landowner supplies the necessary materials (e.g. tree shoots) and bears related expenses (e.g. moving fixtures) while the worker tends the trees for a fixed period. After the expiration of this period, the worker receives a fixed wage or a fixed portion of the orchard.
2. The worker supplies the materials, bears related expenses and receives a share of the harvest. The second more closely resembles *Muzara'a* (c.f.).

Mujtahid

Legal expert or a jurist who expends great effort in deriving a legal opinion or interpreting the sources of *Sharia'a* law.

Murabaha

A contract that refers to the sale and purchase transaction for the financing of an asset whereby the cost and profit margin (mark-up) are made known and agreed to by all parties involved. The settlement for the purchase can be made either on a deferred lump sum basis or on an instalment basis, and is specified in the original agreement.

Musawamah

Musawamah is a sale in which the price of the commodity to be traded is bargained for between the seller and the purchaser without any reference to the price paid or cost incurred by the former.

Musharaka (joint venture financing)

A form of partnership between an Islamic bank and its clients, whereby each party contributes to the capital of the partnership in equal or varying degrees to establish a new project or share in an existing one, and whereby each of the parties becomes an owner of the capital on a permanent or declining basis and is due its share of the profits.

Unlike *Mudaraba*, losses are shared in proportion to the contributed capital. It is not permissible to stipulate alternative loss-sharing arrangements. *Musharaka* is of two types:

Constant Musharaka: This is a *Musharaka* in which the partners' shares in the capital remain constant throughout the period, as specified in the contract.

Diminishing Musharaka: This is a *Musharaka* in which the Islamic bank agrees to transfer gradually to the other partner its (the Islamic bank's) share in the *Musharaka*, so that the Islamic bank's share declines and the other partner's share increases until the latter becomes the sole proprietor of the venture. It is commonly used for Islamic mortgages.

Musaqa

A type of partnership in which the owner of an orchard agrees to share a stipulated portion of the produce of the orchard's trees with a worker, in exchange for the latter's irrigation of the orchard.

Muzara'a

Literally, this means sharecropping. This is an agreement between two parties in which one party agrees to allow a portion of his land to be used by the other party in return for a part of the produce of the land.

Muzabana

Essentially, *muzabana* is a transaction in which the owner of fruit trees agrees to sell his fruit for an estimated equivalent amount of the final produce, such as fruit of the palm, dates or grapes for raisins.

Muzabanah was an agricultural practice known to the people of Medina. It was prohibited by the Prophet ostensibly because of the strong element of *gharar* present in such a transaction. Some *Fuqaha*, particularly *Maliki* jurists, use the term *muzabana* to describe any sale in which the weight or volume of the exchange items is unspecified.

Nisab

The exemption limit for the payment of *zakat*. A Muslim who possesses wealth below the *nisab* is exempted from paying *zakat*, while a Muslim who possesses wealth at or above this exemption limit is obliged to pay *zakat*. The *nisab* differs, depending on the type of wealth in question.

Partnership

This is a term with several types:

> **Contract partnership (sharikat al-'aqd)**: Contract partnership is an agreement between two or more parties to

combine their assets or to merge their services or obligations and liabilities with the aim of making a profit.

Partnership of ownership (sharikat al-milk): Partnership of ownership (*sharikat al-milk*) is the combination of the assets of two or more persons in a manner that creates a state of sharing the realised profit or income or benefiting from an increase in the value of the partnership assets. This combination of assets for making profit also necessitates bearing losses, if any occur.

The ownership partnership is created by events beyond the partners' control such as the inheritance rights of heirs in the legacy of a deceased person. This partnership is also created by the wish of the partners, such as when two or more parties acquire common shares in a particular asset.

Mufawada partnership: *Mufawada* partnership is any partnership in which the parties are equal in all respects, such as funds contributed by them, their right to act and their liability, from the commencement of the partnership to the date of its termination.

Sharecropping partnership: Sharecropping is a partnership in crop cultivation in which one party provides land to another for cultivation and maintenance in consideration for a common defined share in the crop.

Irrigating partnership: Irrigating partnership is a partnership that depends on one party providing designated plants/trees that produce edible fruits to another party who takes responsibility for their irrigation in consideration for a common defined share in the fruits.

Agricultural partnership: Agricultural partnership is a partnership in which one party provides a tree-less piece of land to another to plant trees on it on the condition that they share the revenues from the trees and fruits in accordance with a defined percentage.

See *Mugharasaha, Musaqaha, Muzara'a.*

Qabdh

Qabdh means possession in the context of a contract of exchange. Generally, *qabdh* depends on the perception of '*urf* or the common practices of the local community in recognising that the possession of a good has taken place.

Qard and Qard Hasan

Qard refers to the loan of fungible objects. Legally, *Qard* means to give anything having value for virtuous reasons so that the item/money could provide benefits to the recipient with the condition that the same or similar amount of that thing be paid back on demand or at the agreed time.

The literal meaning of *Qard* is 'to cut.' It is so called because the property is effectively cut-off when it is given to the borrower.

Qard Hasan refers to a benevolent loan. This could be a loan which a person gives to another as help, charity or advance for a certain time period. The repayment of the loan is obligatory. The Prophet is reported to have said '. . . Every loan must be paid . . . .' But if a debtor is in difficulty, the creditor is expected to extend time or even to voluntarily remit the whole or a part of the principal.

It is used as a loan contract between two parties for social welfare or for short-term bridging finance. Repayment is for the same amount as the amount borrowed. The borrower can pay more than the amount borrowed so long as this is not stated in the contract.

Most Islamic banks provide interest-free loans to customers who are in need. The Islamic view of loans (*Qard*) is that there is a moral duty to give them to borrowers free of charge, as a person seeks a loan only if he is in real need of it. Some Islamic banks give interest-free loans only to the holders of investment accounts with them; some extend them to all bank clients; some restrict them to needy students and other economically weaker sections of society; and some provide interest-free loans to small producers, farmers and entrepreneurs who cannot get finance from any other sources.

Qimar

Qimar means gambling. Technically, this is an arrangement in which possession of something of value is contingent upon the happening of an uncertain event. By implication, it applies to a situation in which there is a loss for one party and a gain for the other without specifying which party will lose and which will gain.

Qiyas

Literally, this means measure, comparison or analogy. Technically, it means a derivation of *Sharia'a* law using the analogy of an existing law if the basis (*illah*) of the two laws is the same. It is one of the sources of *Sharia'a* law.

Rahn

This means pledge or collateral. Legally, *Rahn* means to pledge or lodge a real or corporeal property of material value, in accordance with the law, as security for a debt or pecuniary obligation so as to make it possible for the creditor to recover the debt or some portion of the goods or property.

In the pre-Islamic contracts *Rahn* implied a type of earnest money (money guarantees) which was lodged as a guarantee and material evidence or proof of a contract, especially when there was no scribe available to put it into writing.

Restricted Investment Accounts

With this type of account, the investment account holder imposes certain restrictions as to where, how and for what purpose his funds are to be invested, for example, 'Invest my money in Syria.' Further, the Islamic bank may be restricted from commingling its own funds with the restricted investment account funds for investment purposes. In addition, there may be other restrictions which investment account holders may impose. For example, investment account holders may require the Islamic bank not to invest their funds in *Murabaha* instalment sales transactions without guarantor or collateral requirement, or require that the Islamic bank itself should carry out the investment itself rather than do it through a third party.

Riba

This means an excess or increase. Technically, it means an increase over the principal in a loan transaction or in exchange for a commodity accrued to the owner (lender) without giving an equivalent counter value or recompense (*'iwad*), in return, to the other party. *Riba* means an increase which is without an *'iwad* or equal counter value.

Any risk-free or 'guaranteed' rate of return on a loan or investment is *riba*. *Riba* in all its forms is prohibited in Islam.

In Islam, *riba* is one of the most abhorrent of all sins and is absolutely prohibited. *Riba* encompasses various types of illicit gain, of which bank interest is one example.

In conventional terms, *riba* and 'interest' are used inter-changeably, although the legal notion extends beyond mere interest. *Riba* comes in several varieties:

Riba al-Fadl: Also known as *Riba al-Hadith*.

This is a sale transaction in which a commodity is exchanged for an unequal amount of the same commodity and delivery is delayed.

Riba al-Fadl, or *riba* in excess, is the quality premium obtainable when exchanging low quality with better quality goods, for example, dates for dates, wheat for wheat and so on – in other words, an excess in the exchange of *Ribawi* goods within a single genus. The concept of *Riba al-Fadl* refers to sale transactions while *Riba al-Nasiah* refers to loan transactions.

So *Riba al-Fadl* is the *riba* or surplus when exchanging goods. It refers to any commodity-for-commodity exchange transactions (i.e. barter) in which the exchanged commodities are of the same type but of unequal measure, or the delivery of one commodity is postponed.

To avoid *Riba al-Fadl*, the exchange of commodities from both sides must be equal and instant. *Riba al-Fadl* was prohibited by the Prophet Mohammed to forestall *riba* (interest) from creeping into the economy.

Riba al-Nasiah: Also known as *Riba al Qu'ran*.

The usury of debt was an established practice amongst Arabs during the pre-Islamic period. It can occur as an excess or increment in addition to the principal, which is incorporated as an obligatory condition of the giving of a loan.

Alternatively, it occurs when an excess amount is imposed on top of the principal if the borrower fails to repay on the due date. More time is permitted for repayment in return for an additional amount. If the borrower fails to pay again, a further excess amount is imposed and so on.

Riba al-Nasiah, or *riba* of delay, is because of an exchange not being immediate, with or without excess in one of the counter values. It is an increment on the principal of a loan or debt payable. It refers to the practice of lending money for any length of time on the understanding that the borrower would return to the lender at the end of the period, the amount originally lent together with an increase on it, in consideration of the lender having granted him time to pay.

Interest, in all modern conventional banking transactions, falls under the purview of *Riba al-Nasiah*. As money in the present banking system is exchanged for money with excess and delay, it falls under the definition of *riba*. There is a general accord reached among scholars that *riba* is prohibited under *Sharia'a* law.

Ribawi

Goods subject to *Fiqh* rules on *Riba* in sales, variously defined by the schools of *Sharia'a* Law, namely, items sold by weight and by measure, foods and so on. The term is used in the context of items possessing the Islamically unwanted *riba* type characteristics.

Sadaqah

This means charitable giving. This can be compared with *zakat* which is a mandatory tax on Muslims.

Sahih

Literally, in contract law this means sound, healthy or correct. It refers to a valid *Sharia'a* contract and implies a *Hadith* of the highest level of authentication.

Salaf

The word *Salaf* literally means a loan which draws forth no profit for the creditor. In a wider sense, this includes loans for specified periods, that is, short, intermediate and long-term loans. *Salaf* is also another name for *Salam* wherein the price of the commodity is paid in advance while the commodity or the counter value is supplied in the future. The contract creates a liability (debt) for the seller.

Salam

Salam means a contract in which advance payment is made for goods to be delivered later. The seller undertakes to supply some specific goods to the buyer at a future date in exchange for an advance price fully paid at the time of contract.

According to the normal rules of the *Sharia'a*, no sale can be effected unless the goods are in existence at the time of the bargain. However, the *Salam* sale forms an exception, given by the Prophet, to the general rule, provided the goods are defined and the date of delivery is fixed. It is necessary that the quality of the commodity intended to be purchased is fully specified, leaving no ambiguity potentially leading to a dispute. The objects of the *Salam* sale are goods but cannot be gold, silver or currencies.

The latter are regarded as monetary values, the exchange of which is covered under rules of *Sarf*, that is, mutual exchange should be hand to hand without delay. With this latter exception *Salam* covers almost everything which is capable of being definitely described as to quantity, quality and workmanship.

Salam Terminology

Salam is the purchase of a commodity for deferred delivery in exchange for immediate payment according to specified conditions or sale of a commodity for deferred delivery in exchange for immediate payment. The following terms are used for the different parties:

al-Muslam fihi: The commodity to be delivered

al-Muslam ileihi: The seller

al-Muslam: The purchaser

Ra's-almal: Capital (cost) paid (in cash, kind or benefit) in a Salam contract, that is, the price.

Parallel Salam: A *Salam* contract whereby *al-Muslam ileihi* depends, for executing his obligation, on receiving what is due, in the capacity as *al-Muslam*, from a sale in a previous *Salam* contract without making the execution of the second *Salam* contract dependent on the execution of the first one.

Sarf

Basically, in pre-Islamic times this was the exchange of gold for gold, silver for silver and gold for silver or vice versa. Under *Sharia'a* law such exchange is regarded as 'sale of price for price' (*Bai al Thaman bil Thaman*), and each price is in consideration of the other. It also means the sale of monetary value for monetary value, namely, a foreign exchange transaction.

Sharia'a

Alternative spellings include *Sharia*, *Shari'a*, *Shari'ah*, *Syariah*, *Syaria*, *Syari'ah*, *Syari'a*.

The term *Sharia'a* has two meanings: firstly, Islamic law and secondly, the totality of divine categorisations of human acts (Islam). The second meaning of the term is that *Sharia'a* rules do not always function as rules of law in the Western sense, as they include obligations, duties and moral considerations not generally thought of as 'law' in the Western sense. *Sharia'a* rules, therefore, admitting of both a legal and a moral dimension, have as their purpose the fostering of obedience to Allah the Almighty.

In legal terminology, *Sharia'a* means the law as extracted by the *Mujtahid* from the sources of law.

A '*Sharia'a*-compliant' product meets the requirements of Islamic law.

A '*Sharia'a* board' is the committee of Islamic scholars, mandatory for Islamic financial institution, in order to provide guidance and supervision in the development of *Sharia'a*-compliant products.

A '*Sharia'a* advisor' is an independent Islamically trained scholar who advises Islamic institutions on the compliance of products and services with Islamic law.

Sharia'a is Islamic cannon law derived from three primary sources: the *Qur'an*, the *Hadith* and the *Sunnah*.

Shirkah

A contract between two or more persons who launch a business or financial enterprise to make profits. In the conventional books of *Fiqh*, the partnership business may include both *Musharaka* and *Mudaraba*.

Sukuk

Similar to an asset-backed bond, *Sukuk* are forms of commercial paper that provide an investor with ownership in an underlying asset, and a return based on this ownership. The issuing entity needs to identify existing assets to sell to the *Sukuk* investors via transference to a Special Purpose Vehicle

(SPV). The *Sukuk* investors then have a proportionate benefi-cial ownership in these assets. In practice, investors typically take on the credit risk of the issuer rather than real asset risk on the assets owned by the SPV.

Sukuk are certificates, which evidence the undivided pro-rata ownership of underlying assets. The *Sakk* (singular of *Sukuk*) is freely tradable at par, premium or discount.

Sukuk can be listed or unlisted, rated or unrated. *Sukuk* are typically issued by corporate issuers, and some financial insti-tutions and also by Governments (viz, Bahrain, Malaysia and Pakistan).

Sunnah

Literally this means custom, habit or way of life. Technically, this refers to the utterances of the Prophet Mohammed other than those in the *Qur'an*. These are known as the *Hadith*, or his personal acts or sayings of others, all of which were tac-itly approved by the Prophet.

Tabarru'

Literally this means a *Takaful* donation.

It is a contract where a participant agrees to donate a prede-termined percentage of his contribution (to a *Takaful* fund) to provide assistance to fellow participants. In this way, he ful-fils his obligation of joint guarantee and mutual help should another participant suffer a loss. This concept eliminates the element of *gharar* from the *Takaful* contract.

So *Tabarru'* is a donation/gift, the purpose of which is not commercial but given to seek the pleasure of Allah. Any ben-efit that is given by one person to another without getting anything tangible in exchange is called *Tabarru'*.

Takaful

Takaful is Islamic insurance. It is based on the principle of mutual assistance. *Takaful* provides mutual protection of assets and property and offers joint risk-sharing in the event of a loss by one of the participants. *Takaful* is similar to mutual insurance in that members are the insurers as well as the insured.

Takaful is a *Sharia'a*-compliant system of insurance in which the participants donate part or all of their contributions. These are used to pay claims for damages suffered by some of the participants. A *Takaful* company's role is restricted to managing the insurance operations and investing the insurance contributions.

Conventional insurance is prohibited in Islam because its dealings contain several *haram* elements, such as *gharar* and *riba*.

Tapir

Spending wastefully on objects which have been explicitly prohibited by the *Sharia'a*, irrespective of the amount of expenditure.

Tawarruq

This is a reverse *Murabaha*. It is used in personal financing where a client with a genuine need buys an item on credit from a bank on a deferred payment basis and then immediately resells it for cash to a third party. In this way, the client can obtain cash without taking out an interest-based loan.

Unrestricted Investment Accounts

With this type of account, the investment account holder authorises an Islamic bank to invest the account holder's funds in a manner which the Islamic bank deems appropriate, without laying down any restrictions as to where, how and for what purpose the funds should be invested.

Under this arrangement an Islamic bank can commingle the investment account holder's funds with its own funds or with other funds the Islamic bank has the right to use (e.g. current accounts). The investment account holders and the Islamic bank generally participate in the returns on the invested funds. (See *Restricted Investment Accounts.*)

Usufruct

Usufruct is the legal right to use and derive profit or benefit from property that belongs to another person, as long as the property is not damaged. Usufruct originates from civil law, where it is a real right of limited duration on the property of another. The holder of usufruct, known as the usufructuary, has the right to use and enjoy the property, as well as the right to receive profits from the fruits of the property.

The English word *usufruct* derives from the Latin roots *usus* and *fructus*, from verbs meaning *to possess* and *to have the benefit of*, respectively.

The term *fruits* should be understood to mean any replenishable commodity on the property, including (among others) actual fruits, livestock and even rental payments derived from the property.

The term is widely used in the context of *Ijara.*

Wa'd (Promise)

Wa'd is a promise, an obligation issued by one party (in *Murabaha*, the orderer or the purchaser). The promise is binding in *Sharia'a* law on the individual who makes it, the promisor, unless an acceptable excuse arises and prevents its fulfilment. Nevertheless, a promise is binding from the juristic perspective if it is pending on a cause and the promisee has incurred costs by reason of the promise. Mutual promising is a promise against a promise.

Wadi'ah and Wad'iah Yad Dhamanah

Wadi'ah literally means safe custody or safekeeping. Originally safe custody was *Wadiah Yad Amanah*, that is, trustee custody where, according to the *Sharia'a*, the trustee custodian has the duty to safeguard the property held in trust.

Wadi'ah changes to *Wad'iah Yad Dhamanah* (guaranteed custody) when the trustee custodian violates the conditions for safeguarding the property. He then has to guarantee the property.

As *Wadi'ah* is a trust, the depository becomes the guarantor and, therefore guarantees repayment of the whole amount of the deposits, or any part thereof, outstanding in the account of depositors, when demanded. The depositors are not entitled to any of the profits but the depository may provide returns to the depositors as a token of appreciation.

Under this system an Islamic bank acts as the keeper and trustee of depositors' funds. It guarantees to return the entire deposit, or any part of it, on the depositor's demand.

The bank may give the depositor a *hibah* (gift) in appreciation.

Wakala

Wakala means agency. *Wakala* is a standard Islamic practice wherein X (the wakil) acts as the agent of Y. In this capacity, X may execute the affairs of Y. *Wakala* is a widely applicable phenomenon in Islamic finance. It is often used in financial transactions. Whenever a party cannot personally supervise a given affair it deputises another party to execute it on its behalf.

So *Wakala* refers to absolute power of attorney where a representative is appointed to undertake transactions on another person's behalf.

In terms of *Takaful* operations, *Wakala* refers to an agency contract, which may involve a fee for the agent.

Waqf, Awqaf (Pl)

Waqf is a charitable trust. The plural is *Awqaf*. Literally, the word means cessation or detention.

Technically, it refers to the appropriation or tying-up of a property in perpetuity so that no proprietary rights can be exercised over the usufruct. The *waqf* property can neither be sold, nor inherited nor donated to anyone. *Awqaf* consists of religious foundations set up for the benefit of the poor.

Waqf is a standard Islamic transaction in which one 'freezes' property such that it is considered to have been arrested in perpetuity and cannot be sold, inherited or donated. The term *waqf* frequently refers to the property itself. The use of a *waqf* (e.g. a park) is often dedicated to the relief of the poor, the public at large or other charitable ends.

Wasiyah

Will, testament, bequest. The statement of a Muslim in which he details the manner in which his wealth is disposed of after his death.

Zakat

Zakat is a religious tax paid by Muslims. Literally *zakat* means blessing, purification, increase or cultivation of good deeds.

Zakat is an obligatory contribution which every wealthy Muslim is required to pay. The objective is to take away a part of the wealth of the well-to-do and to distribute it among the poor and the needy.

It is a religious obligation of alms-giving, on a Muslim, to pay 2.5% of certain kinds of wealth annually to one of eight categories of needy Muslims.

Zakat is levied on cash, cattle, agricultural produce, minerals, capital invested in industry and business.

There are two types of *zakat*:

- *Zakat al-Fitr*: A small obligatory head tax imposed on every Muslim who has the means. It is paid once yearly at the end of *Ramadan* just before *Eid al-Fitr*. This is also called *Zakat al Nafs* (poll tax).
- *Zakat Al-Mal*: The Muslim's wealth tax. Muslims must pay 2.5% of their yearly savings above a certain amount to the poor and needy Muslims. The *zakat* is compulsory on all Muslims who have saved (at least) the equivalent of 85 g of 24 carat gold at the time when the annual *zakat* payment is due.

Given that *zakat* is levied on different types of wealth there are individual terms for the *zakat* being taxed. These include the following:

Zakatul Huboob: *Zakat* of grain/corn

Zakatul Madan: *Zakat* of minerals

Zakatul Rikaaz: *Zakat* of treasure/precious stones

Zakatul-rid Tijararah: *Zakat* of the profits of merchandise.

Chapter 8

Test Your Knowledge

Having worked through Chapter 4 you are asked to answer as to whether the statements below are true or false.

I Questions

1. *Murabaha* is a type of leasing. **True/False**

2. *Salam* is an investment on the customer's behalf by a bank. **True/False**

3. *Ijara* is a contract whereby the bank buys the goods for the customer and sells them to the customer later. **True/False**

4. *Istisna* is an investment on the customer's behalf by a bank. **True/False**

5. *Salam* is a purchase by a bank whereby the goods are delivered later but the payment is up front. **True/False**

6. *Istisna'a* is a project whereby the bank and an investor both invest capital with both sharing the risks. **True/False**

7. *Mudaraba* is an investment on the customer's behalf by a bank. **True/False**

8. *Murabaha* is a project whereby the bank and an investor both invest capital with both sharing the risks. **True/False**

9. *Istisna'a* is a contract whereby the bank buys the goods for the customer and sells them to the customer later. **True/False**

10. *Murabaha* is a contract whereby the bank buys the goods for the customer and sells them to the customer later. **True/False**

11. *Salam* is a type of leasing. **True/False**

12. *Murabaha* is an order by the bank to manufacture a specific commodity for the purchaser. **True/False**

13. *Istisna'a* is a purchase by a bank whereby the goods are delivered later but the payment is up front. **True/False**

14. *Murabaha* is a purchase by a bank whereby the goods are delivered later but the payment is up front. **True/False**

15. *Mudaraba* is a contract whereby the bank buys the goods for the customer and sells them to the customer later. **True/False**

16. *Musharaka* is a type of leasing. **True/False**

17. *Istisna'a* is an order by the bank to manufacture a specific commodity for the purchaser. **True/False**

18. *Musharaka* is an investment on the customer's behalf by a bank. **True/False**

19. *Mudaraba* is a project whereby the bank and an investor both invest capital with both sharing the risks. **True/False**

20. *Ijara* is a type of leasing. **True/False**

21. *Mudaraba* is a purchase by a bank whereby the goods are delivered later but the payment is up front. **True/False**

22. *Ijara* is an investment on the customer's behalf by a bank. **True/False**

23. *Musharaka* is a project whereby the bank and an investor both invest capital with both sharing the risks. **True/False**

24. *Mudaraba* is an order by the bank to manufacture a specific commodity for the purchaser. **True/False**

25. *Salam* is a project whereby the bank and an investor both invest capital with both sharing the risks. **True/False**

26. *Ijara* is a project whereby the bank and an investor both invest capital with both sharing the risks. **True/False**

27. *Musharaka* is a contract whereby the bank buys the goods for the customer and sells them to the customer later. **True/False**

28. *Ijara* is an order by the bank to manufacture a specific commodity for the purchaser. **True/False**

29. *Murabaha* is an investment on the customer's behalf by a bank. **True/False**

30. *Ijara* is a purchase by a bank whereby the goods are delivered later but the payment is up front.
True/False

31. *Salam* is a contract whereby the bank buys the goods for the customer and sells them to the customer later.
True/False

32. *Musharaka* is an order by the bank to manufacture a specific commodity for the purchaser. **True/False**

33. *Mudaraba* is a type of leasing. **True/False**

34. *Musharaka* is a purchase by a bank whereby the goods are delivered later but the payment is up front.
True/False

35. *Salam* is an order by the bank to manufacture a specific commodity for the purchaser. **True/False**

36. *Istisna'a* is a type of leasing. **True/False**

37. *Musharaka* is a project whereby the bank and a partner both invest capital with the partner taking the risk of capital loss. **True/False**

38. *Mudaraba* is a project whereby the bank and a partner both invest capital with the partner taking the risk of capital loss. **True/False**

39. *Murabaha* is a project whereby the bank and a partner both invest capital with the partner taking the risk of capital loss. **True/False**

40. *Ijara* is a project whereby the bank and a partner both invest capital with the partner taking the risk of capital loss. **True/False**

41. *Istisna'a* is a project whereby the bank and a partner both invest capital with the partner taking the risk of capital loss. **True/False**

42. *Salam* is a project whereby the bank and a partner both invest capital with the partner taking the risk of capital loss. **True/False**

43. *Mudaraba* is a project whereby the bank invests capital and a partner provides managerial expertise, with the bank taking the risk of capital loss. **True/False**

44. *Musharaka* is a project whereby the bank invests capital and a partner provides managerial expertise, with the bank taking the risk of capital loss. **True/False**

45. *Murabaha* is a project whereby the bank invests capital and a partner provides managerial expertise, with the bank taking the risk of capital loss. **True/False**

46. *Istisna'a* is a project whereby the bank invests capital and a partner provides managerial expertise, with the bank taking the risk of capital loss. **True/False**

47. *Ijara* is a project whereby the bank invests capital and a partner provides managerial expertise, with the bank taking the risk of capital loss. **True/False**

48. *Salam* is a project whereby the bank invests capital and a partner provides managerial expertise, with the bank taking the risk of capital loss. **True/False**

What was the score? **?/48**

II Quiz on Islamic Finance Terminology

Fill in the missing words indicated by the figures.

Ijara

Ijara is a form of (1). It involves a contract where the bank (2) and then leases an item – perhaps a consumer durable, for example – to a customer for a specified rental over a specific period. The duration of the lease, as well as the basis for rental, are set and agreed in advance. The bank retains (3) of the item throughout the arrangement and takes back the item at the end.

Ijara-wa-iktina

Ijara-wa-iktina is similar to *Ijara*, except that included in the contract is a (4), at a pre-agreed price. Rentals paid during the period of the lease constitute part of the purchase price. Often, as a result, the final sale will be for a token sum.

Musharaka

Musharaka means partnership. It involves an investor placing his capital with another person with both sharing the (5). The difference between *Musharaka* arrangements and normal banking is that you can set any kind of (6) but losses must be (7) to the amount invested.

Diminishing Musharaka

The principle of diminishing *Musharaka* can be used for home-buying services. Diminishing *Musharaka* means that the bank (8) its equity in an asset with any additional capital payment the customer makes, over and above the (9). The customer's ownership in the asset increases and the bank's (10) by a similar amount each time the customer makes an additional capital payment. Ultimately, the bank transfers ownership of the asset entirely over to the customer.

Mudaraba

Mudaraba refers to an investment on the customer's behalf by a bank. It takes the form of a contract between two parties, one who (11) and the other who (12) and who agrees to the division of any profits made in advance. In other words, the bank would make *Sharia'a*-compliant investments and would share the profits with the customer, in effect charging for the time and effort. If no profit is made, the loss is borne by the customer and the bank takes no fee.

Murabaha

Murabaha is a contract for purchase and resale and allows the customer to make purchases without having to take out a loan and (13). The bank purchases the goods for the customer and (14) them to the customer on a deferred basis, adding an (15). The customer then pays the sale price for the goods over instalments, effectively obtaining credit without paying interest.

Qard

A *Qard* is a loan, free of profit. This is used for Current Accounts. In essence, it means that your Current Account is a (16) to the bank, which is used by the bank for investment and other purposes. Obviously it has to be paid back to you, in full, on demand.

Riba

Riba means interest, which is (17) in Islamic law. Any risk-free or guaranteed interest on a loan is considered to be (18)

Answers

1.
2.
3.
4.
5.
6.
7.
8.
9.
10.
11.
12.
13.
14.
15.
16.
17.
18.

What was your score   ?/18

Chapter 9

Further Reading

ISBN: 978-0-9558351-0-0, 251 pages

Islamic Capital Markets[1]
All you ever need to know about Islamic capital markets. This is the world's first ever book covering the fundamental principles underlying one of the most exciting financial markets.

Reading this book you will learn about capital markets where:

1. Instruments traded are asset backed.
2. Defaults are virtually unknown.
3. A variety of new asset classes are emerging.

Contents of Islamic Capital Markets
Chapter 1. Muslim beliefs

Chapter 2. *Sharia'a* law and *Sharia'a* Boards: roles, responsibility and membership

Chapter 3. Conventional and Islamic financial intermediation

Chapter 4. Islamic capital markets and Islamic securitisation

Chapter 5. Islamic investment principles

---

[1]Available from the author at brian.kettell@islamicbanking courses.com

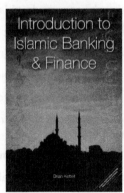

ISBN: 978-0-9558351-1-7, 296 pages

Introduction to Islamic Banking & Finance[2]
An essential first read for anyone interested in Islamic banking, this book covers the principles of the world's fastest growing financial sector. Reading this book you will learn about a banking system where:

---

[2]Available from the author at brian.kettell@islamicbanking courses.com

1. Interest is forbidden.
2. Derivatives are forbidden.
3. Sub-prime mortgages are forbidden.

Contents of Introduction to Islamic Banking & Finance

AAOIFI Publications

The Sharia'a rules and the accounting regulations for Islamic financial institutions are issued by the Accounting and Auditing Association for Islamic Financial Institutions (AAOIFI). These are available from AAOIFI on **www.aaoifi.org**

AAOIFI (1999), *Statement on the Purpose and Calculation of the Capital Adequacy Ratio for Islamic Banks.*

AAOIFI (2004), *Guiding Principles of Risk Management for Institutions (Insurance companies offering only Islamic Financial Services)*.

AAOIFI (2004), *Capital Adequacy Standard for Institutions (offering only Islamic Financial Services)*.

AAOIFI (2008), *Accounting, Auditing and Governance Standards*.

AAOIFI (2008), *Shari'ah Standards*.

References and Further Reading

Abdallah, A. (1987), 'Islamic Banking', *Journal of Islamic Banking and Finance*, 4 (1), 31–56

Abdul, Majid and Abdul, Rais (2003), 'Development of Liquidity Management Instruments: Challenges and Opportunities', paper presented to the *International Conference on Islamic Banking: Risk Management, Regulation and Supervision*, held in Jakarta, Indonesia, 30 September – 2 October 2003, organised by IRTI, Bank Indonesia and Ministry of Finance: Indonesia

Abdul-Rahman, Yahla and Abdulah, S. Tug (1999), 'Towards a LARIBA (Islamic) Mortgage in the United States: Providing an Alternative to the Traditional Mortgages', *International Journal of Islamic Financial Services*, 1 (2), Jul-Sep

Aftab, M. (1986), 'Pakistan Moves to Islamic Banking', *The Banker*, June, 57–60

Aggarwal, R.K. and Yousef, T. (2000), 'Islamic Banks and Investment Financing', *Journal of Money, Credit and Banking*, 32, 93–120

Ahmad, Abdel Rahman Yousri (2001), *Riba, its Economic Rationale and Implications*, New Horizon, No. 109, May-June

Ahmad, Ziauddin (1995), 'Islamic Banking: State of the Art', *IDB Prize Lecture*, Jeddah: Islamic Research and Training Institute, Islamic Development Bank

Alam, M.A. (2000), 'Islamic Banking in Bangladesh: A Case Study of IBBL', *International Journal of Islamic Financial Services*, 1 (4), Jan-Mar

Al-Bashir, M. and al-Amine, Muhammed (2001), 'The Islamic Bonds Market: Possibilities and Challenges', *International Journal of Islamic Financial Services*, 3 (1), Apr-Jun

Al-Jarhi, Mabid Ali and Iqbal, Munawar (2001), 'Islamic Banking: FAQs', *Occasional Paper #4*, Jeddah: Islamic Research and Training Institute

Ali, Syed Ameer (1978), *The Spirit of Islam: A History of the Evolution and Ideals of Islam, with a Life of the Prophet*, London: Chatto & Windus

al-Misri, Ahmad ibn Naqid (1988), *Reliance of the Traveller: A Classical Manual of Islamic Sacred Law*, Translation by Nuh Ha Mim Keller

Al-Qaradawi, Yusuf (1985), *The Lawful and the Prohibited in Islam*, Islamic Book Trust: Kuala Lumpur, Malaysia

Al-Suwailem, Sami (2000), 'Decision Under Uncertainty, An Islamic Perspective', in *Islamic Finance: Challenges and Opportunities in the Twenty-First Century (Conference Papers)*, Loughborough: Fourth International Conference on Islamic Economics and Banking

Anouar, H. (2002), 'Profitability of Islamic Banks', *International Journal of Islamic Financial Services*, 4 (2), Jul-Sep

Archer, Simon and Karim, Rifaat Abdel (2002), *Islamic Finance: Innovation and Growth*, London: Euromoney Books and AAOIFI

Archer, S., Karim, R. Abdel, and Al-Deehani, T. (1998), 'Financial Contracting, Governance Structures and the Accounting Regulation of Islamic Banks: An Analysis in Terms of Agency Theory and Transaction Cost Economics', *Journal of Management and Governance*, 2, 149–170

Ariff, M. (1982), 'Monetary Policy in an Interest-Free Islamic Economy – Nature and Scope', in Ariff, M. (ed.), *Monetary and Fiscal Economics of Islam*, International Centre for Research in Islamic Economics: Jeddah

Ariff, Mohammad and Mannan, M.A. (1990), *Developing a System of Islamic Financial Instruments*, Jeddah: Islamic Research and Training Institute

Armstrong, Karen (2002), *Islam: A Short History* (revised edn.), New York: Modern Library

Ayub, Muhammad (1995), 'Meaning of Riba', *Journal of Islamic Banking and Finance*, 12 (2)

Ayub, Mohammad (2007), *Understanding Islamic Finance*. John Wiley

Babikir, Osman Ahmed (2001), *Islamic Financial Instruments to Manage Short-term Excess Liquidity*, Research Paper No. 41, 2nd edn., Jeddah: Islamic Research and Training Institute

Bacha, O.I. (1999), 'Financial Derivatives: Some Thoughts for Reconsideration', *International Journal of Islamic Financial Services*, 1 (1), Apr-Jun

Baldwin, K. (2002), 'Risk Management in Islamic Banks', in Karim, R. Abdel and Archer, S. (eds.), *Islamic Finance: Innovation and Growth*, Euromoney Books and AAOIFI, pp. 176–197

Basel Committee on Banking Supervision (BCBS) (2003), *Consultative Document – Overview of the New Basel Capital Accord*, Bank for International Settlements

Bashir, A. (1996), 'Profit-sharing Contracts and Investment under Asymmetric Information', *Research in Middle East Economics*, 1, 173–186

BenDjilali, Boualem and Khan, Tariqullah (1995), *Economics of Diminishing Musharakah*, Jeddah: IRTI

Bowker, John (1999), *What Muslims Believe*, Oxford, UK: OneWorld

Buckmaster, Daphne (ed.) (1996), 'Central Bank Supervision: The Need for Unity', in *Islamic Banking: An Overview*, Institute of Islamic Banking and Insurance: London, pp. 143–145

Buckmaster, Daphne, (ed.) (1996), 'Alternative Tools of Supervision by Central Banks', in *Islamic Banking: An Overview*, Institute of Islamic Banking and Insurance: London, pp. 146–150

Burton, John (1990), *The Sources of Islamic Law: Islamic Theories of Abrogation*, Edinburgh: Edinburgh University Press

Burton, John (1994), *An Introduction to the Hadith*, Edinburgh: Edinburgh University Press

Chapra, M. Umer (1982), *'Money and Banking in an Islamic Economy'*, in Ariff, M. (ed.)

Chapra, M.U. (1985), *Towards a Just Monetary System*, Islamic Foundation

Chapra, M.U. (1992), *Islam and the Economic Challenge*, Islamic Foundation

Chapra, M.U. (2000), *The Future of Islamic Economics*, Islamic Foundation

Chapra, M. Umer (2000), 'Why has Islam Prohibited Interest?: Rationale Behind the Prohibition of Interest', *Review of Islamic Economics*, 9

Chapra, M. Umer and Ahmed, Habib (2002), *Corporate Governance in Islamic Financial Institutions*, Occasional Paper #6, Jeddah: Islamic Research and Training Institute

Chapra, M. Umer and Khan, Tariqullah (2000), *Regulation and Supervision of Islamic Banks*, Occasional Paper No. 3, Jeddah: Islamic Development Bank – Islamic Research and Training Institute

Cook, Michael (2000), *The Koran: A Very Short Introduction*, Oxford, UK: Oxford University Press

Cooter, Robert and Ulen, Thomas (2000), *Law and Economics*, 3rd edn., Reading MA: Addison-Wesley

Coulson, N.J. (1994), *A History of Islamic Law*, Edinburgh University Press

Cunningham, A. (2001), *Culture of Accounting: What are the Real Constraints for Islamic Finance in a Riba-Based Global Economy?* Moody's Investor Services, London: UK

Dale, Richard (2000), 'Comparative Models of Banking Supervision', paper presented to the *Conference on Islamic Banking Supervision*, Bahrain: AAOIFI, February

Dar, H.A. and Presley, J.R. (1999), 'Islamic Finance: A Western Perspective', *International Journal of Islamic Financial Services*, 1 (1), Apr-June

Dar, H.A. and Presley, J.R. (2000), 'Lack of Profit Sharing in Islamic Banking: Management and Control Imbalances', *International Journal of Islamic Financial Services*, 2 (2), Jul-Sep

De Lorenzo, Yusuf Talal (eds.) (1997), *A Compendium of Legal Opinions on the Operations of Islamic Banks: Murabaha, Mudaraba and Musharaka*, Institute of Islamic Banking and Insurance: London, UK

El-Din, A.K. (1986), 'Ten Years of Islamic Banking', *Journal of Islamic Banking and Finance*, 3 (3), 49–66

El-Gamal, Mahmoud (2000), 'An Economic Explication of the Prohibition of *Gharar* in Classical Islamic Jurisprudence', in *Islamic Finance: Challenges and Opportunities in the Twenty First Century (Conference Papers)*, Loughborough: Fourth International Conference on Islamic Economics and Banking

El-Gamal, M.A. (2003), *Financial Transactions in Islamic Jurisprudence*, Vols 1 and 2, Translation of Book by Dr. Al-Zuhayli

El-Gamal, M.A. (2006), *Islamic Finance: Law, Economics and Practice*, Cambridge University Press

Elgari, M. Ali (1997), 'Short Term Financial Instruments Based on *Salam* Contracts', in Ahmad, Ausaf and Khan, Tariqullah (eds.), *Islamic Financial Instruments for Public Sector Resource Mobilization*, Jeddah: Islamic Research and Training Institute, pp. 249–266

El-Karanshawy, Hatem (1998), 'CAMEL Ratings and their Relevance for Islamic Banks', paper presented to a *Seminar on Islamic Banking Supervision , organised by the Arab Monetary Fund*: Abu Dhabi

El Sheikkh, Fath El Rahman (2000), 'The Regulation of Islamic Banks by Central Banks', *The Journal of International Banking Regulation*, Fall(2000), 43–49

Errico, Luca and Farahbaksh, Mitra (1998), 'Islamic Banking: Issues in Prudential Regulations and Supervision', *IMF Working Paper 98/30*, Washington: International Monetary Fund

Esposito, John L. (1995), *The Oxford Encyclopedia of the Modern Islamic World*, 4 Vols. Oxford, UK: Oxford University Press

Fadeel, Mahmoud (2002), 'Legal Aspects of Islamic Finance', in Archer, Simon and Karim, Rifaat Abdel (eds.), *Islamic Finance: Growth and Innovation*, Euromoney Books, London: UK

Gafoor, A.L.M. Abdul (2001), *Mudaraba-based Investment and Finance*, New Horizon, No. 110, July

Gafoor, A.L.M. Abdul (2001), *Riba-free Commercial Banking*, New Horizon, No. 112, September

Garrett, R. and Graham, A. (eds.) (1998), *Islamic Law and Finance*, *Introduction* by William Ballantyne, London: Graham & Trotman Limited

Grais, W. and Kantur, Z. (2003), *The Changing Financial Landscape: Opportunities and Challenges for the Middle East and North Africa*, *World Bank Policy Research Working Paper 3050*, May 2003

Hallaq, Wael B. (ed.) (2003), *The Formation of Islamic Law*, Aldershot: Ashgate

Haque, Nadeemul and Mirakhor, Abbas (1999), 'The Design of Instruments for Government Finance in an Islamic Economy', *Islamic Economic Studies*, 6 (2), 27–43

Haron, S. and Ahmad, Norafifah (2000), 'The Effects of Conventional Interest Rates on Funds Deposited with Islamic Banking System in Malaysia', *International Journal of Islamic Financial Services*, 1 (4), Jan-Mar

Haron, Sudin and Shanmugam, Bala (1997), *Islamic Banking System: Concepts and Applications*, Pelanduk Publications: Selangor, Malaysia

Hassan, Sabir Mohammad (2000), 'Capital Adequacy and Basel Guidelines: On Risk Weights of Assets for Islamic Banks', paper presented at the *Conference on the Regulation of Islamic Banks*, Bahrain, February

Henry, C.M. and Wilson, Rodney (eds.) (2004), *Politics of Islamic Finance*, Edinburgh University Press

Homoud, S. (1985), *Islamic Banking*, Graham & Trotman Publication

Hoque, M.Z. and Choudhury, Masdul Alam (2003), 'Islamic Finance: A Western Perspective Revisited', *International Journal of Islamic Financial Services*, 4 (4), Apr-June

Ibrahim, Tag El-Din S. (1991), 'Risk Aversion, Moral Hazard and Financial Islamization Policy', *Review of Islamic Economics*, 1 (1)

Iqbal, Zamir (1997), 'Islamic Financial Systems', *Finance and Development (IMF)*, 34 (2), June

Iqbal, Z. (2001), 'Profit and Loss Sharing Ratios: A Holistic Approach to Corporate Finance', *International Journal of Islamic Financial Services*, 3 (2), Jul-Sep

Iqbal, M. (ed.) (2002), *Islamic Banking and Finance*, Leicester, UK: The Islamic Foundation

Iqbal, M. and Khan, Tariqullah (2005), *Financial Engineering and Islamic Contracts*, Palgrave-Macmillan

Iqbal, Munawar and Llewellyn, David T. (2002), *Islamic Banking and Finance: New Perspectives in Profit Sharing and Risk*, London: Edward Elgar Publishers

Iqbal, Zubair and Mirakhor, Abbas (1987), *Islamic Banking*, IMF Occasional Paper No. 49, Washington, DC: International Monetary Fund

Iqbal, Z and Mirakhor, Abbas (2007), *An Introduction to Islamic Finance: Theory and Practice*, John Wiley

Iqbal, Zamir and Mirakhor, Abbas (2002), 'Development of Islamic Financial Institutions and Challenges Ahead', in Archer, Simon and Karim, Rifaat Abdel (eds.) *Islamic Finance: Growth and Innovation*, Euromoney Books, London: UK

Iqbal, M. and Molyneux, Philip (2005), *Thirty Years of Islamic Banking: History and Performance*, Palgrave-Macmillan

Iqbal, Munawar *et al.* (1999), *Challenges Facing Islamic Banking*, Jeddah: IRTI, Occasional Paper #2

Islamic Fiqh Academy of the Organization of Islamic Conference (1989), *Islamic Fiqh Academy Resolutions and Recommendations*, Jeddah

Jaffer, S. (ed.) (2004), *Islamic Asset Management: Forming the Future for Sharia-Compliant Investment Strategies*, Euromoney

Kahf, Monzer (1994), 'Time Value of Money and Discounting in Islamic Perspectives Revisited', *Review of Islamic Economics*, 3 (2)

Kahf, Monzer (1996), 'Distribution of Profits in Islamic Banks', *Studies in Islamic Economics*, 4 (1)

Kahf, Monzer (1997), 'The Use of Assets *Ijarah* Bonds for Bridging the Budget Gap', in Ahmad, Ausaf and Khan, Tariqullah (eds.), *Islamic Financial Instruments for Public Sector Resource Mobilization*, Jeddah: Islamic Research and Training Institute, pp. 265–316

Kahf, Monzer and Khan, Tariqullah (1992), *Principles of Islamic Financing*, Jeddah: IRTI

Kamali, Mohammad Hashim (2000), *Principles of Islamic Jurisprudence*, revised edn, Cambridge, UK: The Islamic Texts Society

Kamali, H. (2003), *Islamic Commercial Law: An Analysis of Futures and Options*, Islamic Texts Society

Karim, Rifaat Ahmed Abdel (2001), 'International Accounting Harmonization, Banking Regulation and Islamic Banks', *The International Journal of Accounting*, 36 (2), 169–193

Karsten, I. (1982), 'Islam and Financial Intermediation', *IMF Staff Papers*, 29 (1), 108–142

Kettell, B. (2001), *Economics for Financial Market*, Butterworth's-Heinemann

Kettell, B. (2001), *Financial Economics*, Financial Times-Prentice Hall

Kettell, B. (2002), *Islamic Banking in the Kingdom of Bahrain*, Bahrain Monetary Agency (BMA)

Kettell, B. (2007), *Islamic Sukuk: A Definitive Guide to Islamic Structured Finance*. Available from the author

Kettell, B. (2008), *Introduction to Islamic Banking and Finance*. Available from the author on brian.kettell@islamicbankingcourses.com

Kettell, B. (2009), *Islamic Capital Markets*. Available from the author

Kettell, B. (2010), *Islamic Banking in Nutshell*, John Wiley

Khan, W.M. (1985), *Towards an Interest-Free Islamic Economic System*, The Islamic Foundation, Leicester, UK

Khan, Mohsin S. (1986), 'Islamic Interest-Free Banking: A Theoretical Analysis', *IMF Staff Papers*, 33 (1), 1–27

Khan, M. (1987), 'Islamic Interest-Free Banking: A Theoretical Analysis', in Khan, Mohsin S. and Mirakhor, Abbas (eds.), *Theoretical Studies in Islamic Banking and Finance*, The Institute of Islamic Studies: TX, USA, pp. 15–36

Khan, M.F. (1991), *Comparative Economics of Some Islamic Financing Techniques*, Research Paper No. 12, Jeddah: Islamic Research and Training Institute, Islamic Development Bank

Khan, Tariqullah (1995), 'Demand for and Supply of PLS and Mark-up Funds of Islamic Banks – Some Alternative Explanations', *Islamic Economic Studies*, 3 (1), IRTI

Khan, M. Fahim (1996), *Islamic Futures and their Markets*, Jeddah: IRTI

Khan, M.F. (1999), 'Financial Modernisation in the Twenty-First Century and Challenges for Islamic Banking', *International Journal of Islamic Financial Services*, 1 (3), Oct-Dec

Khan, M.Y. (2001), 'Banking Regulations and Islamic Banks in India: Status and Issues', *International Journal of Islamic Financial Services*, 2 (4), Jan-Mar

Khan, Tariqullah and Ahmad, Habib (2001), *Risk management: an analysis of issues in the Islamic financial industry*, Jeddah: IRTI, Occasional Paper #5

Khan, Tariqullah and Habib, Ahmad (2001), *Risk Management: An Analysis of Issues in the Islamic Financial Industry*, Jeddah: IRTI Occasional Paper #5

Khan, Mohsin and Mirakhor, A. (1986), 'The Framework and Practice of Islamic Banking', *Finance and Development*, September

Khan, Mohsin S. and Mirakhor, A. (1992), 'Islam and the Economic System', *Review of Islamic Economics*, 2 (1), 1–29

Khan, Mohsin and Mirakhor, Abbas (1993), 'Monetary Management in an Islamic Economy', *Journal of Islamic Banking and Finance*, 10, Jul-Sep, 42–63

Lewis, Mervyn K. and Algaoud, Latifa M. (2001), *Islamic Banking*, Edward Elgar: Cheltenham, UK

Maroun, Y. (2002), 'Liquidity Management and Trade Financing', in Karim, R. Abdel and Archer, S. (eds.), *Islamic Finance: Innovation and Growth*, Euromoney Books and AAOIFI, pp. 163–175

Mills, Paul S. and Presley, John R. (1999), *Islamic Finance: Theory and Practice*, London: Macmillan

Mirakhor, Abbas (1995), 'Theory of an Islamic Financial System' in *Encyclopaedia of Islamic Banking*, London: Institute of Islamic Banking and Finance

Moore, Philip (1997), *Islamic Finance: A Partnership for Growth*, Euromoney Publications PLC: London, UK

Mulajawan, D., Dar, H.A., and Hall, M.J.B. (2002), *A Capital Adequacy Framework for Islamic Banks: The Need to Reconcile Depositors' Risk Aversion with Managers' Risk Taking, Economics Research Paper*, pp. 02–13, Loughborough University

Naughton, S.A.J. and Tahir, M.A. (1988), 'Islamic Banking and Financial Development', *Journal of Islamic Banking and Finance*, 5 (2)

Nienhaus, V. (1983), 'Profitability of Islamic PLS Banks Competing with Interest Banks: Problems and Prospects', *Journal of Research in Islamic Economics*, 1 (1), 37–47

Nienhaus, V. (1986), 'Islamic Economics, Finance and Banking – Theory and Practice', *Journal of Islamic Banking and Finance*, 3 (2), 36–54

Norman, A.A. (2002), 'Imperatives for Financial Innovation for Islamic Banks', *International Journal of Islamic Financial Services*, 4 (2), Oct-Dec

Obaidullah, Mohammad (1998), 'Capital Adequacy Norms for Islamic Financial Institutions', *Islamic Economic Studies*, 5 (1,2)

Obaidullah, Mohammad (1998), 'Financial Engineering with Islamic Options', *Islamic Economic Studies*, 6 (1), IRTI, IDB

Obaidullah, Mohammad (1999), 'Islamic Financial Options: Potential Tools for Risk Management', *Journal of King Abdulaziz University (Islamic Economics), Saudi Arabia*, 11, 3–28

Obaidullah, Mohammad (2000), 'Regulation of Stock Markets in an Islamic Economy', *Proceedings of the Third International Conference on Islamic Banking and Finance*, August, Loughborough University, Leicester, UK

Obaidullah, Mohammad (2001), 'Ethics and Efficiency in Islamic Stock Markets', *International Journal of Islamic Financial Services*, 3 (2), Jul-Sep

Obaidullah, Mohammad (2001), 'Financial Contracting in Currency Markets', *International Journal of Islamic Financial Services*, 3 (3), Oct-Dec

Obaidullah, Mohammad (2002), 'Islamic Risk Management', *International Journal of Islamic Financial Services*, 3 (4), Jan-Mar

Presley, John R. and Sessions, John, G. (1993), 'Islamic Economics: The Emergence of a New Paradigm', *Journal of Economic Theory*, 1994

Qami, I.H. (1995), 'Regulatory Control of Islamic Banks by Central Banks', in *Encyclopaedia of Islamic Banking and Insurance*, Institute of Islamic Banking and Insurance: London, pp. 211–215

Rahman, Yahia Abdul (1994), *Interest Free Islamic Banking – Lariba Bank*, Al-Hilal Publishing, Kuala Lumpur

Rahman, Y.A. (1999), 'Islamic Instruments for Managing Liquidity', *International Journal of Islamic Financial Services*, 1 (1), Apr-Jun

Rosly, S.A. (2005), *Critical Issues in Islamic Banking and Financial Markets*, Bloomington, IN

Rosly, A.R. and Sanussi, Mohammed M. (1999), 'The Application of Bay-al-Inah and Bai-al-Dayn in Malaysian Islamic Bonds: An Islamic Analysis', *International Journal of Islamic Financial Services*, 1 (2), Jul-Sep

Roy, O. (2004), *Globalised Islam, The Search for a New Ummah*, Huot & Co. Publishers

Saleh, Nabil A. (1992), *Unlawful Gain and Legitimate Profit in Islamic Law*, 2nd edn., London, UK: Graham and Trotman

Salehabadi, A. and Aram, M. (2002), 'Islamic Justification of Derivative Instruments', *International Journal of Islamic Financial Services*, 4 (3), Oct-Dec

Sarker, M.A.A. (1999), 'Islamic Business Contracts: Agency Problems and the Theory of Islamic Firms', *International Journal of Islamic Financial Services*, 1 (2), Jul-Sep

Sarwar, A.A. (1995), 'Islamic Financial Instruments: Definition and Types', *Review of Islamic Economics*, 4 (1), 1–16

Shirazi, H. (1990), *Islamic Banking Contracts*, Butterworth-Heinemann, Taleghani, Sayyid Mahmood

Siddiqi, M.N. (1983), *Issues in Islamic Banking*, The Islamic Foundation

Siddiqi, M.N. (1985), *Partnership and Profit Sharing*, The Islamic Foundation

Siddiqi, M.N. (1988), *Banking Without Interest*, The Islamic Foundation

Sundararajan, V. and Errico, L. (2002), 'Islamic Financial Institutions and Products in the Global Financial System: Key Issues in Risk Management and Challenges Ahead', *IMF working paper, IMF/02/192*, Washington, DC: International Monetary Fund

Sundararajan, V., Marston, David, and Shabsigh, Ghiath (1998), 'Monetary Operations and Government Debt Management under Islamic Banking', *WP/98/144*, Washington, DC: IMF

Udovitch, Abraham (1970), *Partnership and Profit in Early Islam*, Princeton, NJ: Princeton University Press

Udovitch, Abraham L. (1970), *Partnership and Profit in Medieval Islam*, Princeton, NJ: Princeton University Press

Udovitch, Abraham L. (1981), *Bankers Without Banks: Commerce, Banking and Society in the Islamic World of the Middle Ages*, Princeton Near East Paper No. 30, Princeton, NJ: Princeton University Press

Usmani, Muhammad Taqi (1998), *An Introduction to Islamic Finance*, Karachi: Idaratul Ma'arif

Usmani, M.T. (2000), *The Historic Judgment on Interest*, Idaratul-Ma'arif, Karachi

Uzair, Mohammad (1955), *An Outline of 'Interestless Banking'*, Karachi: Raihan Publications

Uzair, Mohammad (1982), 'Central Banking Operations in an Interest-Free Banking System', in Ariff, M. (ed.)

Vogel, Frank E. and Hayes, Samuel L. (1988), *Islamic Law and Finance: Religion, Risk and Return*, The Hague: Kluwer Law International

Warde, I. (2000), *Islamic Finance in the Global Economy*, Edinburgh: University Press

Zaher, T. and Hassan, K. (2001), 'A Comparative Literature Survey of Islamic Finance and Banking', *Financial Markets, Institutions and Instruments*, 10 (4), 155–199

WEB SITE ADDRESSES

www.islamicbanking courses.com	**The website for the authors training courses and publications**
http://finance.groups.yahoo.com/group/ibfnet	**Islamic Business & Finance Network**. One of the most popular and active Islamic financial networks.
http://islamic-finance.net/journal.html	*International Journal of Islamic Financial Services* (an electronic academic refereed Journal).
www.islamicfi.com	**General Council for Islamic Banks & Financial Institutions** (An International organization for banks in Islamic countries.)
www.isdb.org	**The Islamic Development Bank Group**. A multilateral International organization to foster social and economic development for member countries, based in Jeddah, Saudi Arabia. The present membership of the Bank consists of 58 countries.
http://www.irti.org/	**Islamic Research & Training Institute (IRTI)**. The Institute publishes *Islamic Economic Studies* (An academic refereed journal) in addition to numerous studies, books, monographs, conferences.

http://www.worldwaqf.org/	**World Waqf Foundation** (An Islamic international trust organization).
www.islamic-foundation.org.uk	Based in the UK, it hosts the **International Association of Islamic Economics**. The Association publishes *Review of Islamic Economics* (An academic refereed journal).
www.iaie.net	**The International Association of Islamic Economics**.
http://www.aaoifi.com	**Accounting & Auditing Organization of Islamic Financial Institutions (AAOIFI)**. The Organization is widely recognised by central banks, Islamic banks, and other international organizations.
www.difc.ae	**The Dubai International Financial Centre (DIFC) is** the world's newest international financial centre. It aims to develop the same stature as New York, London and Japan.
http://www.ifp.harvard.edu	**Islamic Finance Project:** part of **The Islamic Legal Studies Program at Harvard University**. The *Project* has been organizing an annual conference on Islamic finance and economics since 1997.

www.cbb.gov.bh	**Central Bank of Bahrain (CBB)**. Bahrain is the most important centre for Islamic financial services in the world. This site contains lots of information about Islamic Banking.
www.lmcbahrain.com	**Liquidity Management Centre** for Islamic financial institutions, based in Bahrain. The Centre aims at developing and deepening the secondary market for Islamic financial assets.
www.bnm.gov.my	**Bank Negara Malaysia** (the Central Bank of Malaysia). The site contains data about Islamic banking in Malaysia.
www.sbp.org.pk/index.cfm	**State Bank of Pakistan**. The site contains data about Islamic banking in Pakistan.

Other useful sites

http://www.icmif.org/

http://islamic-finance.net/

http://monzer.kahf.com/index.html

http://www.kazi.org/

www.islamicbookstore.com

www.islamic-banking.com

http://kitaabun.com/shopping3/

www.halalco.com/economics.html

www.islamic-economics.com

www.islampub.com/books/econom.html

www.siddiqi.com/mns

http://www.ruf.rice.edu/~elgamal/files/islamic.html

www.islamonline.net

www.islamicfi.com

www.aibim.com.my

www.islamicbankingnetwork.com

www.islamicbanking-finance.com/facts.html

www.riba-free-banking.com

www.dfm.co.ae

www.adsm.co.ae

http://islamicity.com/finance/IslamicBanking_Evolution.html

http://islamiccenter.kau.edu.sa/english/publications/publications.html

http://islamiccenter.kau.edu.sa/english/Publications/Obaidullah/ifs/ifs.html

http://www.Islamicbankingcourses.com

http://www.iiff.com/index.cfm/page/content/contentid/118/menuid/111

http://en.wikipedia.org/wiki/Ijtihad

http://www.islamicfinancenews.com

http://www.cibafi.org

http://islamic-finance.net

http://site.securities.com

http://www.arabfinancialforum.org/

http://www.ruf.rice.edu/~elgamal/files/interest.pd

http://www.djindexes.com/jsp/islamicMarket.jsp?sideMenu=true

http://www.aibim.com.my

Islamic Banking Crossword

Fill in all the boxes

ACROSS

- 4 A follower of Islam
- 6 Islamic leasing
- 8 Ship of the desert
- 9 Arabic money
- 13 Uncertainty in Islam
- 16 The Arabic name for God
- 18 Capital city of Bahrain
- 19 Islamic law
- 20 Pillar of Islam
- 22 Multilateral development bank in Jedda (acronym)
- 24 Nature of Islamic calendar
- 26 Islamic holiday
- 27 Religious leader in the Muslim community
- 29 Saying of the Prophet
- 30 Pillar of Islam
- 32 Religious ruling

- 33 Dominant sect in Iran
- 37 Forbidden in Arabic
- 38 Source of rules governing daily life of Muslims
- 40 Language of prayer
- 41 Place of worship
- 42 Profit share technique
- 43 Capital city of Oman

DOWN

- 1 The nation of Islam
- 2 Pillar of Islam
- 3 Location of the two holiest sites in Islam (two words)
- 5 An Arab chief
- 7 Largest Islamic banking centre
- 10 Permissible in Arabic
- 11 Excess

- 12 The Sacred House
- 14 Capital city of Qatar
- 15 Holiest book in Islam
- 17 Islamic accounting body
- 21 Holiest city in Islam
- 23 Cost-plus sale
- 25 Capital city of Saudi Arabia
- 27 To submit
- 28 Partnership mode of finance
- 31 Forbidden chops
- 33 Dominant sect in Islam
- 34 Forward sale contract
- 35 Project financing technique
- 36 Islamic insurance
- 38 Islamic Bond
- 39 To struggle and strive to practise Islam

Solution:

Appendix

Answers to Chapter 8 Test Your Knowledge

Questions

1. *Murabaha* is a type of leasing. **False**

2. *Salam* is an investment on the customer's behalf by a bank. **False**

3. *Ijara* is a contract whereby the bank buys the goods for the customer and sells them to the customer later. **False**

4. *Istisna'a* is an investment on the customer's behalf by a bank. **False**

5. *Salam* is a purchase by a bank whereby the goods are delivered later but the payment is up front. **True**

6. *Istisna'a* is a project whereby the bank and an investor both invest capital with both sharing the risks. **False**

7. *Mudaraba* is an investment on the customer's behalf by a bank. **True**

8. *Murabaha* is a project whereby the bank and an investor both invest capital with both sharing the risks. **False**

9. *Istisna'a* is a contract whereby the bank buys the goods for the customer and sells them to the customer later. **False**

10. *Murabaha* is a contract whereby the bank buys the goods for the customer and sells them to the customer later. **True**

11. *Salam* is a type of leasing. **False**

12. *Murabaha* is an order by the bank to manufacture a specific commodity for the purchaser. **False**

13. *Istisna'a* is a purchase by a bank whereby the goods are delivered later but the payment is up front. **False**

14. *Murabaha* is a purchase by a bank whereby the goods are delivered later but the payment is up front. **False**

15. *Mudaraba* is a contract whereby the bank buys the goods for the customer and sells them to the customer later. **False**

16. *Musharaka* is a type of leasing. **False**

17. *Istisna'a* is an order by the bank to manufacture a specific commodity for the purchaser. **True**

18. *Musharaka* is an investment on the customer's behalf by a bank. **False**

19. *Mudaraba* is a project whereby the bank and an investor both invest capital with both sharing the risks. **False**

20. *Ijara* is a type of leasing. **True**

21. *Mudaraba* is a purchase by a bank whereby the goods are delivered later but the payment is up front. **False**

22. *Ijara* is an investment on the customer's behalf by a bank. **False**

23. *Musharaka* is a project whereby the bank and an investor both invest capital with both sharing the risks. **True**

24. *Mudaraba* is an order by the bank to manufacture a specific commodity for the purchaser. **False**

25. *Salam* is a project whereby the bank and an investor both invest capital with both sharing the risks. **False**

26. *Ijara* is a project whereby the bank and an investor both invest capital with both sharing the risks. **False**

27. *Musharaka* is a contract whereby the bank buys the goods for the customer and sells them to the customer later. **False**

28. *Ijara* is an order by the bank to manufacture a specific commodity for the purchaser. **False**

29. *Murabaha* is an investment on the customer's behalf by a bank. **False**

30. *Ijara* is a purchase by a bank whereby the goods are delivered later but the payment is up front. **False**

31. *Salam* is a contract whereby the bank buys the goods for the customer and sells them to the customer later. **False**

32. *Musharaka* is an order by the bank to manufacture a specific commodity for the purchaser. **False**

33. *Mudaraba* is a type of leasing. **False**

34. *Musharaka* is a purchase by a bank whereby the goods are delivered later but the payment is up front. **False**

35. *Salam* is an order by the bank to manufacture a specific commodity for the purchaser. **False**

36. *Istisna'a* is a type of leasing. **False**

37. *Musharaka* is a project whereby the bank and a partner both invest capital with the partner taking the risk of capital loss. **False**

38. *Mudaraba* is a project whereby the bank and a partner both invest capital with the partner taking the risk of capital loss. **False**

39. *Murabaha* is a project whereby the bank and a partner both invest capital with the partner taking the risk of capital loss. **False**

40. *Ijara* is a project whereby the bank and a partner both invest capital with the partner taking the risk of capital loss. **False**

41. *Istisna'a* is a project whereby the bank and a partner both invest capital with the partner taking the risk of capital loss. **False**

42. *Salam* is a project whereby the bank and a partner both invest capital with the partner taking the risk of capital loss. **False**

43. *Mudaraba* is a project whereby the bank invests capital and a partner provides managerial expertise, with the bank taking the risk of capital loss. **True**

44. *Musharaka* is a project whereby the bank invests capital and a partner provides managerial expertise, with the bank taking the risk of capital loss. **False**

45. *Murabaha* is a project whereby the bank invests capital and a partner provides managerial expertise, with the bank taking the risk of capital loss. **False**

46. *Istisna'a* is a project whereby the bank invests capital and a partner provides managerial expertise, with the bank taking the risk of capital loss. **False**

47. *Ijara* is a project whereby the bank invests capital and a partner provides managerial expertise, with the bank taking the risk of capital loss. **False**

48. *Salam* is a project whereby the bank invests capital and a partner provides managerial expertise, with the bank taking the risk of capital loss. **False**

What was the score? ?/48

II Quiz on Islamic Finance Terminology

Fill in the missing words indicated by the figures.

Ijara

Ijara is a form of **(1) LEASING.** It involves a contract where the bank **(2) BUYS** and then leases an item – perhaps a consumer durable, for example – to a customer for a specified rental over a specific period. The duration of the lease, as well as the basis for rental, are set and agreed in advance. The bank retains **(3) OWNERSHIP** of the item throughout the arrangement and takes back the item at the end.

Ijara-wa-Iktina

Ijara-wa-Iktina is similar to *Ijara*, except that included in the contract is a **(4) PROMISE FROM THE CUSTOMER TO BUY THE EQUIPMENT AT THE END OF THE LEASE PERIOD**, at a pre-agreed price. Rentals paid during the period of the lease constitute part of the purchase price. Often, as a result, the final sale will be for a token sum.

Musharaka

Musharaka means partnership. It involves an investor placing his capital with another person with both sharing the **(5) RISK AND RETURN**. The difference between *Musharaka* arrangements and normal banking is that you can set any kind of **(6) PROFIT SHARING RATIO** but losses must be **(7) PROPORTIONATE** to the amount invested.

Diminishing *Musharaka*

The principle of diminishing *Musharaka* can be used for home-buying services. Diminishing *Musharaka* means that the bank **(8) REDUCES** its equity in an asset with any additional capital payment the customer makes, over and above the **(9) RENTAL PAYMENTS.** The customer's ownership in the asset increases and the bank's **(10) DECREASES** by a similar amount each time the customer makes an additional capital payment. Ultimately, the bank transfers ownership of the asset entirely over to the customer.

Mudaraba

Mudaraba refers to an investment on the customers behalf by a bank. It takes the form of a contract between two parties, one who **(11) PROVIDES THE FUNDS** and the other who

(12) PROVIDES THE EXPERTISE and who agrees to the division of any profits made in advance. In other words, the bank would make *Sharia'a*-compliant investments and would share the profits with the customer, in effect charging for the time and effort. If no profit is made, the loss is borne by the customer and the bank takes no fee.

Murabaha

Murabaha is a contract for purchase and resale and allows the customer to make purchases without having to take out a loan and **(13) PAY INTEREST.** The bank purchases the goods for the customer and **(14) SELLS** them to the customer on a deferred basis, adding an **(15) AGREED PROFIT MARGIN.** The customer then pays the sale price for the goods over instalments, effectively obtaining credit without paying interest.

Qard

A *Qard* is a loan, free of profit. This is used for Current Accounts. In essence, it means that your Current Account is a **(16) LOAN** to the bank, which is used by the bank for investment and other purposes. Obviously it has to be paid back to you, in full, on demand.

Riba

Riba means interest, which is **(17) PROHIBITED** in Islamic law. Any risk-free or guaranteed interest on a loan is considered to be **(18) USURY**.

Index

Printed and bound by CPI Group (UK) Ltd, Croydon, CR0 4YY

16/04/2025

14658824-0001